Tracking the Gods

Marie-Louise von Franz, Honorary Patron

**Studies in Jungian Psychology
by Jungian Analysts**

Daryl Sharp, General Editor

Tracking the Gods

The Place of Myth
in Modern Life

JAMES HOLLIS

For Jill, whose love for me,
and whose secure sense of self,
allows and supports me
to do these things which are necessary.

For Taryn and Tim, Jonah and Seah,
children always present.

And for "Terry," who tried to eat the sun ...

Canadian Cataloguing in Publication Data

Hollis, James, 1940-
    Tracking the Gods: the place of myth in modern life

(Studies in Jungian psychology by Jungian analysts; 68)

Includes bibliographical references and index.

ISBN 978-0-919123-69-4

1. Myth-Psychological aspects.
2. Jung, C.G. (Carl Gustav), 1875-1961.
I. Title. II. Series.

BL313.H65 1995   291.1'3'019   C95-930074-0

INNER CITY BOOKS
53 Alvin Ave., Toronto, ON M4T 2A8, Canada.
Telephone (416) 927-0355
Toll-free in Canada and U.S.: 1-888-927-0355
www.innercitybooks.net / booksales@innercitybooks.net

Honorary Patron: Marie-Louise von Franz.
Publisher and General Editor: Daryl Sharp.
Senior Editor: Victoria B. Cowan.
Office Manager: Scott Milligen.
IT Manager: Sharpconnections.com.
Social Media: Tasha Tollman.
Editorial Assistance: David Sharp, J. Morgan, E. Jefferson.

Cover: "Oracle," acrylic on canvas, by Vicki Cowan (© 1994).

Index by Daryl Sharp

Printed and bound in Canada by Thistle Printing Limited

Contents

Introduction
Because Being Here Amounts To So Much

> Why . . .
> have a yearning for destiny?
> . . . because being here amounts to so much, because all
> this Here and Now, so fleeting, seems to require us and strangely
> concerns us. Us the most fleeting of all . . . .
> Having been once on earth—can it ever be canceled?
> —Rainer Maria Rilke, "The Ninth Duino Elegy."

Wherever they first gathered, from swirling desert sands to frost-caked tundra, from great oceans to primeval forests and high plateaus, the questions were there with them: Who are we? How did we get here? Where are we going?—repeated in tongues, scratched on walls of caves and hides of beasts, enacted in recurrent patterns attending the passage of seasons, the solemn rites of birth and death, war and love-making. Always the questions were there.

Today, these questions haunt us still. If there is anything that distinguishes the human species from others, it is the endurance of such questions, our power to ask them, and our need to locate ourselves in the great rhythms of change and continuity.

Jungian writers are sometimes puzzling to general readers, not to mention their colleagues in other schools of psychology, because of their references to myth. They frequently borrow from legend, and while there may be some aesthetic appeal in those stories, why they would be helpful to us psychologically may remain obscure. At best Jungians, and their interest in myth, are tolerated; at worst they are considered fuzzy brained and, gasp, crypto-mystics. This book is an effort to explain why Jungian psychology has so frequently been nourished by myth and, more important, why the study of myth is critical for us as individuals and as citizens of our age.

Myth takes us deep into ourselves and into the psychic reservoirs of humanity. Whatever our cultural and religious background or personal psy-

7

chology, a greater intimacy with myth provides a vital linkage with meaning, the absence of which is so often behind the private and collective neuroses of our time. Expressed in its most succinct form, the study of myth is the search for that which connects us most deeply with our own nature and our place in the cosmos. Surely no more central issue confronts us collectively and individually.

Our culture has lost the longitudes and latitudes of the soul, hence our crazed careening from ideology to ideology. Even the concept of myth has been degraded to the status of falsehood. "Oh, that's just a myth," we say. Yet we who seek to understand, to deepen, are obliged to recover an opening to myth which then permits myth to open to us.

The Greek word *mythos* means *word, story, speech,* related to the notion of expression. But expression of what? What myth ultimately expresses is the human take on things, that is, the imposition of dramatic structures on the flux and chaos of nature. Quite possibly, nature has no inherent meaning; it simply is. But humans bring a psychic structuring process, which is part of our nature, to that chaos in order to establish a meaningful relationship to the world. Myth, with its substance of symbol, rhythm and metaphor, bridges from the unknown to the knower and helps the human stand in some sort of meaningful relationship to mystery. Myth has a mediatorial function, as implied by the etymology of symbol and metaphor *(syn + ballein,* to project toward sameness, and *meta + pherein,* to carry over or across).

By definition we cannot know the mysteries, but we are driven by our nature to stand in meaningful relationship to them. (The first sentence of Aristotle's *Metaphysics* is "All men, by nature, desire to know.") The images of myth, when drawn from the depths, stir and touch us even when we do not know why, because they intimate, even activate, the mysterious depths we embody as well. Myth then resonates because it intimates what we already carry in our nature but can only dimly perceive by cognition.

Many of us were inured to the voice of myth by early exposure to Greek or Judeo-Christian myth. We were badly served by teachers or clerics who construed them as interesting but faded narratives of a remote past, or insisted that we accept as literal what offended common sense. Perhaps such purveyors of myth had themselves never tumbled to the resonant depths of mythic materials; whatever, they damaged myth for us. Both trivialization and literalism are egregious affronts to the soul. Both miss the point.

The soul (Greek πσψχηε or *psyche*) expresses itself through image but is not that image. As Sören Kierkegaard reminded us, "The god which can be named is not God."[1] The dynamic incarnation of soul through the image manifests this mysterious energy. When we resonate to this incarnated energy, we know we are in the presence of soul. When, for whatever reason, the energy no longer enlivens that image for us, then that structure dies for us as a source of the divine. There remains but a dead myth or ritual that touches us not. This is how a god or an entire religious institution can die. The energy has departed, leaving a dry husk.

So it is with us—life energy enters us at conception, mysteriously, and departs, mysteriously, leaving only a husk. What is living in a symbol, a myth or a person is the divine energy, not the vessel. Thus we see how our teachers and religious leaders misunderstood. To see myth simply as interesting old stories is to say that the energy that once entered those images and rendered them luminous has now departed, seeking incarnation elsewhere. To literalize a myth or symbol and require its worship, on the other hand, is the oldest of religious sins: idolatry. The mystery the image once contained is now lost and one worships an empty shell no longer worthy of adoration. When the image (that is, the symbol) no longer points beyond itself to the precincts of mystery, then it is dead. But the mystery lives on, elsewhere. (We shall track where that mystery has gone, where the energy now incarnates, in our last chapter.)

Given this understanding of the mediatorial function of symbol or mythic image, one can see how critical such images are, for they help us stand in a human relationship to the mystery. As finite creatures, we cannot appropriate or understand the infinite, and yet we are obliged to establish a standpoint vis-à-vis mystery. The mediatorial image is the bridge between self and world, self and other, even self and self. Our respect is for the mystery not the bridge. Therefore, every mythic tradition, every religious institution, if it is to properly serve the mystery, should relinquish

---

[1] *Concluding Unscientific Postscript,* vol. 1, p. 291.

its images from time to time. The anxiety we feel in the face of change and ambiguity leads us to cling to known symbols, but continuing to worship them is to pay disrespect to the mystery, which is already elsewhere.

Fundamentalism is the sin of literalism. It is blasphemous because it seeks to limit the autonomy of divine energy to what can be known and contained. This may lower anxiety but is contrary to the very nature of mystery. The anxiety of ambiguity seeks to limit the autonomy of mystery by fixing the image; the fixation of image is literalism; literalism is idolatry. The truly religious attitude toward life obliges us to suffer ambiguity, ride the current of soul as it changes and disappears, and await its reappearance in a fresh place. What else is faith, then, but iconoclasm, and the strength to wait upon the mystery?

It is easy enough to track such energy historically, for an image that seizes and transforms the soul of an entire culture can quickly reify and grow lifeless. The anxiety that individuals or cultures feel at that moment is considerable and they may quickly grasp hold of a new image in order to feel secure again. Since humankind can bear little existential angst, there naturally emerge ideologies and fads, fashions and affectations, which momentarily assuage anxiety. I know a man who at last count had purchased eighty-eight automobiles. I know a woman who has passed from cult to cult, ideological fashion to ideological fashion, as if a new idea, like a new dress, might cover the yawning abyss.

I recall an audience member once asking Joseph Campbell, that great student of myth, "Do you believe in God?" "Which one," he responded, "there have been hundreds of thousands, you know." Immediately we were transported to a different plane. From the questioner's urgency to fix the god, to define the concept and thereby lessen the psychic distress, we had been reminded that not only are the Immortal Ones mortal, but that the God-imagos wax and wane like the moon, except their cycles may be more millennial than monthly.

On a personal level, we all cling to images of ourselves, images of another era, images lent by culture or parents, images outgrown, irrelevant, constrictive. In my book *The Middle Passage,* I noted that we work very hard to construct an adaptive sense of self, with a history, a set of attitudes toward self and others, and a series of reflexive responses whose purpose is to reduce our existential angst. Much of this assembled self is derived from childhood experience, reinforced by the effects of cultural conditioning. The natural self is buried beneath this acquired self, resulting in self-estrangement and sundry symptoms of dis-ease. By midlife the natural self often threatens to overthrow the shaky sovereignty of the provisional personality. This occasions distress and confusion as one clings to an antiquated self-image. But clinging to one's old sense of self is stultifying to the impulses of individuation, so the distress only grows. In effect, because of the anxiety of letting go of the known, one is attaching oneself to a dead myth.

Constrained as it is within a false imago, the soul suffers. We may not know why we feel such distress, but we suffer and often occasion suffering in others. The soul, embodiment of the mysterious energies that drive the cosmos, no longer feels at home in the old symbol system we think of as our personality, our emotional center. It suffers the loss of what Jung called variously the divine drama and the symbolic life. Meaning only comes, he said,

> when people feel that they are living the symbolic life, that they are actors in the divine drama. That gives the only meaning to human life; everything else is banal and you can dismiss it. A career, producing of children, all are *maya* [illusion] compared with that one thing, that your life is meaningful.[2]

Just as religious faith obliges one to wait with trust in the mystery, so the evolution of the personality, the individuation urge toward wholeness, obliges one to wait upon, and trust the guidance of, the soul's energies. The enemy of such trust is the anxiety occasioned by ambiguity. As one matures, a greater tolerance of ambiguity is essential both for growth and as a measure of respect for the autonomy of the mystery.

If we are describing as mythic in character phenomena as distinctly different as a narrative from the ancient Near East and a person's ego-concept, then we are obviously employing the concept of myth rather broadly. What unites both examples is that meaningful images have been energized. Similarly, the energy animating the image can depart and leave a culture or

---

[2] "The Symbolic Life," *The Symbolic Life,* CW 18, par. 630. [CW refers throughout to C.G. Jung, *The Collected Works]*

an individual lifeless. Perhaps a definition of myth that embraces these disparate realities is: *Myth is the dramatization of conscious or unconscious values of a group or an individual.*

The critical factor of this definition is that the images are dynamic, whether they stand separately or are part of a narrative tissue. Such energy can animate any form that is shapeable. Images can manifest in words, movement, plastic arts, science, architecture, or any other form of cultural or personal expression. In other words, anything that can carry the imprint of divine energies can be a temporary vessel of the mysteries, or the gods.

Our experience of these meaningful events may be conscious or unconscious; what matters is that they touch us, moving us to transcendent or bestial ends. Any of the ten thousand things of the world that can be bent to our soul's intent and upon which the mysterious energy has left its mark may be considered mythic in character. Thus, our art and religions for sure, but also our popular culture, our cityscapes—all bear the trace of soul. Whether individuals or groups were conscious of this myth-making event is irrelevant, as is whether the implicit values are experienced by the group or the individual. What matters is how the person is linked to or disconnected from that which brings depth and meaningful movement in life.

Consider our architecture, for example, something remote from our general sense of myth. Steel and glass and concrete are malleable and carry the imprint of our psychic structures. If a wanderer were to come across our cities in a thousand years, what would he or she think of our values, our rituals, our social character? Might that wanderer conclude that we, back there in the so-called twentieth century, were a pragmatic, function-oriented group that cared little for beauty, for space, for community? Note the crammed and cramped spaces, the uniformity, the depersonalization of our cities, and conclude we cared for commerce, speed and function but little for the freedom of organic life? From such cultural artifacts they might discern both the modernist achievement and disfigurement of soul.

Just as today's anthropologists seek to reconstruct the sensibility of previous cultures, so future generations will seek to understand the kind of world we have made for ourselves. They will ask the same questions of us that we ask of the past, and we can ill afford to be less conscious of our values than those who one day will sift through our bones and cerements.

The Services of Myth

Joseph Campbell identified four ways in which myth serves human need. Each office of myth is an imaginal speculation upon the character of our relationship with the four orders of mystery—to the cosmos, to nature, to each other and to ourselves. While no myth addresses all four, each addresses at least one of these great questions.

The cosmological question

Like our tribal ancestors, even as children we asked, "How did I get here? Who, or what, was here before, and will be after? Why?"

Such questions are natural, for knowing who we are requires some sense of our point of departure and our destiny. The cosmological office of myth addresses the questions of ultimacy, of genesis and eschatology, alpha and omega. It matters whether one sees random chaos, absurdity,the unfolding of natural law, or a guiding intelligence and comprehensible plan behind the universe, because such conclusions help locate the person in a context of meaning. If one feels that the universe is absurd and devoid of meaning, then the burden of meaning falls directly upon the shoulders of the individual.

If meaning is not implicit in the structures of nature and the evolution of history, then it is clearly the task of humans to render their lives meaningful through the quality of their choices. If one posits the reality of gods, what is their nature? Their relationship to us? Are they detached or involved, and do they possess a morality? Does living well in this world then imply discerning the will of the gods and aligning ourselves with it, or is there a place for a differentiation between the will of the gods and the drives of humanity? (In "Answer to Job," Jung went so far as to suggest that humans play a vital role in the moral development, the spiritual evolution, of God.)[3] Or is it even possible for mortal beings to talk meaningfully about such matters without literalizing their finite projections onto the Infinite or slipping into anthropomorphic delusion?

Each tribal entity, each civilization, has its account of beginnings, of

---

[3] See *Psychology and Religion: West and East,* CW 11, pars. 553ff., and Edward F. Edinger, *Transformation of the God-Image: An Elucidation of Jung's* Answer to Job.

first things, of impersonal forces of nature at work, of benevolent or malign deities at sport or purposive intent, of unfathomable mysteries whose precincts cannot be approached. If we are tempted to smile with a trace of condescension at some of these accounts, we should remind ourselves that each represents a profound effort to make sense of the cosmos, to stand in relationship to it, to mediate its terrors and appropriate its beauty. Such efforts go on in the early life of the child and of civilizations, and if we look back and discern a misreading of the evidence, nonetheless we still must attend our place and direction in the vast and rolling cosmos. Otherwise our species remains adrift and alone. Those who in their adulthood have stopped pondering their relationship to the cosmos may revel in superficial distractions, but their angst, their natural curiosity and need for meaning persist and trouble sleep.

The metaphysical question

Metaphysics is the effort to identify the nature of reality, especially the nature of the world around us, the nature of Nature. What is our relationship to what archetypally is called "the Great Mother," out of whose womb we come and to whose bosom we return? We are drawn to such anthropomorphic imagery because, again, we are trying to establish a human relationship to the mystery.

I once taught in a college in a forest, in the province of Pan, six miles from the haunt of Poseidon, whose mascot was the endangered osprey. Daily I consume the broken body of the goddess Ceres in my morning cereal, sacrifice Protean foods to my stomach and end up in the Land of Nod. Such images were once charged with energy. The gods were both numinous (from Latin *numen*, magical or spell-binding) and luminous; they shone forth from the world of natural phenomena. Some of that energy still lingered into the nineteenth century when Baudelaire wrote:

> nature is a temple from whose living columns
> commingling voices emerge at times;
> Here man wanders through forests of symbols
> which seem to observe him with familiar eyes.[4]

---

[4] "Correspondences," in Angel Flores, trans., *An Anthology of French Poetry from de Nerval to Valéry*, p. 21.

Anyone who gets close to the ocean feels the presence of primal power. One is gripped by Poseidon whether that god comes to mind or not. A person who wanders astray in the trackless forest of the soul will similarly be gripped by the resident god Pan(ic). Such images have by and large lost their numinosity; their energy has gone elsewhere, subsumed by the mundane. We are the ones bereft. Since the beginning these symbols have helped to establish a bridge between human sensibility and those experiences that lie beyond our cognitive powers. Three eminent men of science—Darwin, Jung and William James—separately experienced an earthquake and reflexively turned to the same imagery, writing in their journals that they felt as if they were astride a huge dragon that threatened to throw them off. Again, metaphor helps mediate the awesome and the awful. When it is missing, we suffer disconnection. Moderns may be able to manipulate natural forces and genetic codes, but compared to the ancients we have a sterile contact with mystery.

The sociological question

As our ancestors groped toward each other in the primal night, communities arose not only for food gathering, division of labor and collective defense, but for still deeper purposes. They sought community not only out of loneliness and fear, powerful as those emotions are, but also for sharing, for enlargement, for mutuality. Who one is is in part defined by *whose* one is—to whom or to what communal purpose one subscribes.

Social organization serves biological needs, for sure, but it also serves the spirit. Meaning comes to the individual through participation in the tribal experience. A group of people who come together for a defined purpose, food gathering for example, is a society, loosely bound and subject to fragmentation under pressure. It only becomes a community when a collective experience—natural, cultural or supernatural—lifts each person out of isolation into an encounter with a transcendent or transpersonal reality. Then the individual is not only a member of a society organized for a specific function, but also a participant in a dimension which defines that person in relationship to the transcendent. Clearly, self-identity derives not only from personal life and cooperative efforts. A relationship to the past (time as *chronos*) enables one to participate also in the eternal (time as *kairos*). Thus, for example, Jesus is dead, but the Christian believes that

Christ lives in him or her and in every moment.

The original experience of mystery was phenomenological in character, beyond understanding or articulation—for instance a god speaking from a burning bush, a great migration prompted by a leader's dream. Out of such encounters with archetypal powers, images emerge to mediate the gulf. However, symbols that initially point beyond themselves toward the primal experience reify with the passage of time; they deteriorate into signs or icons which no longer point toward the mystery but divert primal experience into ossified concept. Indeed, the difficulty of regaining access to the primal experience which helped define the community haunts history.

Three cultural artifices are employed to seek reconnection with the primal mysteries—dogma, rites and cultic practices. *Dogma* represents the afterthought of a people as they seek to contain the mystery by the power of thought, by the stratagems of scripture, theology and catechism. *Rites* are symbolic reenactments of the primal experience. *Cultic practices* help define the singularity of one group versus another by the way they dress, interact, and incarnate their tribal response to the demands of everyday life. All of these are well-meaning attempts to sustain the primacy of original experience, but few survive the erosion of time.

Thus dogma can evolve into assertions that neither touch nor speak to subsequent generations. Rites can lose their exemplary power and luminosity. Cultic practices can deteriorate into habit, oppressive tradition, even a tyranny of expectations. Similarly, institutions formed to preserve and promulgate the impact of the primal encounter with mystery, be they religious, educational or political, often become oppressive, preventing us from personally experiencing the mystery, finally serving only their own self-preservation. History is not kind to even timeless experiences.

Yet out of these socialized encounters with the mysteries humans often find great meaning, and much of their definition of what it means to be a human in their particular time or place. Addressing the specifics of social life—how we relate to each other, the ministries of love and of war, where the individual fits in the context of collectivity—consumes much of an individual's journey. We have Freud reminding us that the inevitable price of civilization is neurosis, and Thomas Mann concluding that the destiny of the modern is worked out in the political forum. How one is to contribute to and draw from the commonwealth while still being oneself has been and remains the hammer and anvil of the human enterprise wherein soul may be foiled or forged.

The psychological question

Just as the association with others assists our survival and supports our need for community, so membership in the group exacts a price which sometimes jeopardizes the psychological integrity of the individual. How we are to understand ourselves as ourselves is the psychological task of myth. Literally, this means asking questions such as: "Who am I? How am I to conduct my life? What is my proper place in the world, my vocation? How am I to find a companion who is right for me?"

Cultures with vital mythic images support the individual in attaining a sense of self, facilitate maturation and guide social interaction. A culture that has lost its mythic center, or whose mythologies are too fragmented and diverse, creates frightened and lost people who drift from cult to cult, ideology to ideology. Living symbols, however, can initiate us into the mysteries of our own soul.

No single myth can address all four of these great challenges, but all mythic structures embody responses to one or more of them. The fact that the implicit mythic values may be so camouflaged in the artifacts of pop culture or daily life as to be unrecognized by consciousness does not prevent them from exercising a profound influence on both the individual and the collective psyche.

The function of myth, therefore, is to initiate the individual and/or the culture into the mysteries of the gods, the world, society and oneself.

Differing Approaches to Myth

Today there is a renewed interest in myth, in part because we feel that, as Blaise Pascal noted in the seventeenth century, "we wander in times which are not ours," or we share Hamlet's sense that "the time is out of joint," or agree with Rilke that "we are not much at home in the world we have created."[5]

---

[5] Pascal, *Pensées,* no. 172, p. 49; Shakespeare, *Hamlet,* act 1, scene 5, line 189; Rilke, *Duino Elegies,* no. 1, lines 11-12.

This renewed interest began in the nineteenth century as industrialization and urbanization separated many from their psychic heritage. Not all theories of myth honor the psychological implications, but the review presented below will illustrate their wide range.

1. Antiquarian

This view of myth acknowledges our natural curiosity about other peoples, especially our ancestors. Not only are we naturally curious about others, we also seek to know ourselves better by understanding how our predecessors addressed the four great questions mentioned above. The myths they left behind represent the architecture of their sensibility. If we understand myth only as an antiquarian artifact, however, we may overlook the contribution the past may make to widening our own sense of the range of human possibilities. T.S. Eliot concluded that our only superiority to the past derived from our capacity to include it as part of our present.[6] We may also miss the depth at which the mythic images resonate in the timeless zones of the psyche, a place where past and present are yet one.

2. Sociological

This reading of myth sees it as the carrier of the social values of a group. Whether St. George actually slew the dragon or whether the walls of Jericho really fell to the sound of a horn is beside the point. What matters are the values a society desires to affirm and the standards chosen to define them. The social values carried dynamically in a myth say more about the intentions of a culture, even its capacity for self-delusion, than about how people really live their lives. In examining the sociological character of myth, then, we are discerning how that particular culture differentiates itself from others in the unique way it addresses the four great questions common to human experience.

3. Historical

The historical understanding of myth sees the narratives of gods and heroes as faded accounts of real people and real events, however trans-

---

[6] "Tradition and the Individual Talent," in Hagard Adams, ed., *Critical Theory Since Plato,* p. 78.

formed through the alchemy of time, oral transmission and imaginative embellishment. When von Schliemann found the ancient city of Troy and the alleged mask of Agamemnon, he added nothing to the grandeur of the Homeric vision, which stands on its own merits, though he did add a touch of excitement for those who believe myths have some basis in historic fact. But whether a myth is based on a specific place, person or event is fundamentally irrelevant to its larger testimony to the permutations of the human spirit.

4. Proto-scientific

Many understand myth as the inadequate reading of nature—what humans had before science. They forget that the motifs of science are also mythological. They think the mystery we call gravity, for example, is comprehensible simply because we have named it. They think that quarks, quasars and black holes have some more objective status than Ares and Aphrodite. They forget that scientists knowingly employ fictions, models of reality readily supplanted by more useful ones. They forget that great leaps of conjecture and the subjective nature of all knowledge are implicit even in the most "objective" of assertions.

In the foundation myths of all peoples we see attempts to humanize natural phenomena as a way of standing in human relationship to the mysteries. In the Sumerian creation story, for example, the mingling of Mumu and Tiamat may very well recall the emergence of the fertile crescent from the confluence of the Tigris and Euphrates rivers. But to see myth as only proto-science is to miss the point. Nothing we say about the mysteries has much to do with the mysteries themselves, lest they not be mysteries; such assertions derive rather from the imaginal, subjective state out of which the human has always sought to make the universe intelligible.

5. Anthropological

The anthropologist is concerned with the origins and rise of human culture. In the body of culture produced by any tribal unit, in the rites and cultic practices of a civilization, one may witness primal paths of access to the mysteries. The rending of the sacrificial animal becomes in time the tearing turmoil of tragedy. Rites of blood and baptism attending birth, initiation, kinship changes and death give form and purpose to the otherwise absurd transit of mortality. In the recovery of ancient myth and rite, we may track the gods, discern primal metaphors that give some sense of how others stood in relationship to the mysteries. The Christian Eucharist, for example, is a later version of an old idea, the eating of the gods. Through the act of faith, even the flesh is sanctified, infused with mana, and one ingests the divine.

6. Linguistic

The etymological study of a word, concept or mythologem will often lend considerable insight into the root metaphor which arose to express the inexpressible primal experience. We gain deeper understanding of the Hebrew mythopoeic imagination, for example, if we know that etymologically the name *Adam* meant "of the earth" and *Eve* meant "living." So, too, our imaginal capacity is quickened when we learn that the word *tragedy* derives from "goat-song." What these root metaphors imply about the human in relationship to the divine illumines our own experience.

7. Psychological

Immanuel Kant observed two centuries ago that we can never know the world or objects in themselves, only our subjective experience of them. Jung went a few steps further in asserting that all human experience is essentially psychoid, that is, has both mental and material components. The crossing point of all lines of outer and inner experience is in the human psyche. Moreover, we are constantly projecting our psychic life onto the screen of the world around us. We see in the smudge of an ink blot the outlines of a citadel, a tree, a devil, a fiddler on the roof. We see in other people aspects we admire or despise in ourselves. We depict in our stories and songs aspects of our own inner life.

Accordingly, many students of myth have read them as a fascinating thesaurus of scenarios that dramatize the processes of psychological life. Freud and Freudians especially borrowed such myths as Oedipus and Electra to illustrate the recurrent themes that drive humans. In such use, and sometimes misuse, of myth, one may see the instinctual desires and value conflicts of the individual and often of the tribe as well. This approach to myth understands it as a demonstration of the universality of psychological functioning.

8. Archetypal

This view of myth arose from the work of C. G. Jung. In his first clinical posting at the Burgholzli Klinik in Zürich he worked with numerous schizophrenics. Rather than dismiss the products of these minds in turmoil, Jung made a concerted effort to understand their psychological meaning. He found that often, no matter how distorted the imagery, there was a mythic kernel which had great meaning in the context of the life of the patient.

To understand such imagery better, Jung undertook massive, life-long research into the treasure-house of images that had accumulated down through history, from Eastern mysticism to medieval alchemy, from Christianity to aboriginal beliefs. He discovered that certain motifs recurred throughout world culture and also in dreams and other psychic phenomena experienced by individuals.

Quite apart from the transmission of images from one culture to another, which often could be proved not to have happened, he concluded that all humans possessed a similar psychic structuring process. This process is grounded in nature and is as instinctual as eating and sleeping. Its apparent purpose is to bring about greater meaning by imposing pattern upon chaos. These recurrent motifs he called archetypes, a word whose etymology suggests "primal imprint" or "pattern" but which may also usefully be seen as a verb rather than a noun. The psyche archetypes, that is, structures, the stuff of daily life into motifs that give form and meaning to life. Consciousness does not invent such patterns; it experiences them as though they have come from another place whose familiarity strangely moves us.

Jung further speculated that all humans exercise this structuring process, and that the autonomous activity of soul employs such motifs as number, object, process and the like, no matter the idiosyncrasies of a particular individual or culture. The content of the archetype is of course filled with personal elements, but the formative pattern is impersonal and universal. Beneath the level of consciousness lies the personal unconscious, which is comprised of all that a particular individual has experienced. But beneath that level of the psyche is the collective unconscious, where each of us participates in the universal experience we call human. Jung came to decipher much of the content of the psychotic's experiences, for in those motifs one could find not only universal elements but what psychic process looks like without the provisional veneer of local culture or personality. In examining the dreams of a modern person, for example, the images may arise from twentieth-century culture, yet the forms, movement and motifs are to be found in earlier cultures as well.

Some years ago I taught a year-long course on myth using Joseph Campbell's four-volume study, *The Masks of God*. It was the eleventh out of sixteen sessions before we reached the rise of Judaism and the thirteenth before the start of Christianity. By that point the participants had two reactions. They felt overwhelmed and rather insignificant in light of what had transpired before the beginnings of what we call Western culture, but they also saw that they had already encountered in earlier cultures nearly all the motifs they had naively thought unique to ours. Seeing the archetypal movements in history humbled them but also communicated the timeless universality of human experience.

The hero archetype, for example, may be acted out in diverse ways. Those who make headlines, an Odysseus or Copernicus, a Beethoven or Lindbergh, are formal carriers of the aspirations of a people, but the unsung heroics of ordinary Jane and Joe in the process of understanding themselves are no less archetypally based. Whether the hero archetype manifests on a collective or an individual level, it attests to the universal human need to expand the limits of the possible.

9. Phenomenological

Myth is a form of radical apprehension (radical, from Latin *radix*, root). We may think rationally, but thinking is derivative, a secondary process. We experience phenomenologically, as a felt movement of body and soul. All primal encounters are apprehended mythologically, as when the men of science mentioned above experienced an earthquake as a gigantic beast. Those who have primal encounters, such as falling in love or witnessing the birth of their child, know that ordinary concepts are inadequate to the task of understanding. On such occasions we "think in our bones" or "feel in our gut."

Myths are dramatically experienced portraits, in whatever form or medium; they move below the realm of consciousness even as consciousness seeks to define and control an experience that is larger than the powers of cognition.

10. Symbolic

As may be clear by now, myth represents the crystallization of basic experiences of life construed through various forms of imagery. Such imagery lies beyond intellectual comprehension yet is experienced meaningfully. Mythic images help us to approach the mysteries. Myth draws us near the profound depths of love and hate, life and death—precincts of the gods, the mysteries, where categories of thought falter and slip into dumbfounded silence. Myth is a way of talking about the ineffable.

Pascal once wrote, "The silence of these empty spaces frightens me."[7] Myth is a way of continuing the conversation when the awesome silence gathers. In theory and system one sees the language of mind; in myth one sees the incarnate language of the soul.

Reading myth, then, is a form of personal and cultural psychotherapy (Greek *psyche,* soul, and *therapeuein,* to listen or attend to). Thus psychotherapy, whether it takes place in an analyst's office or in the mindful attention to one's inner life, is "listening to the soul." The recurrent motifs of myth constitute the movement of soul through the ages and through the life of the individual.

---

[7] *Pensées,* no. 206, p. 61.

1
The Rag-and-Bone Shop of the Heart

The Mythos of Modernism

Toward the end of his life, W. B. Yeats, the great poet of modernism, surveyed his career and the mythic dismantlement of his epoch, and concluded:

> Now that my ladder's gone,
> I must lie down where all ladders start,
> In the foul rag-and-bone shop of the heart.[8]

The "ladder" here is a metaphor for the hierarchical values that historically the artist could presume. When Sophocles or Shakespeare dramatized a value conflict, they could assume a relatively stable set of ranked values in the culture over against which the players and the audience could take their mythic mark. The erosion of those implicit, and often explicit, normative values leaves the artist without external points of reference. With mythic longitudes and latitudes removed, the soul is adrift and the artist is left to forge anew the conscience of the race, in the smithy of his soul, as James Joyce put it,[9] or in the affective center, the rag-and-bone shop of the heart. Decades earlier, Matthew Arnold had noted that the modern is "wandering between two worlds, one dead, / the other powerless to be born."[10] This in-betweenness is what most characterizes modernism. As Martin Heidegger put it, we live in the time "between the Gods which have fled, and the Gods which are not yet."[11]

One could say that the last time the Western world made collective sense, that is, when king and commoner alike could agree—"Yes, here is what the world means, here are the agreed-upon values, and here is our

---

[8] "The Circus Animal's Desertion," in *Collected Poems of W.B. Yeats,* p. 335.

[9] *Portrait of the Artist as a Young Man,* in *The Portable James Joyce,* p. 526.

[10] "Stanzas from the Grand Chartreuse," in *Poetry and Criticism of Matthew Arnold,* p. 187.

[11] "Hölderlin and the Essence of Poetry," in *Existence and Being,* pp. 288-289.

accepted genesis and eschatology"—was somewhere around 1320. By the time Dante's *Divine Comedy* appeared, with its vision of a three-tiered cosmos, its hierarchical ladder of moral cause and consequence, the consensus it incarnated had already begun to erode. With the Black Death of 1348-49, which obliterated some forty per cent of the population of Europe—and with it, many of the salvationist claims of the Church—and the subsequent rise of mercantile, capital-based bourgeois culture and the secular humanism we now call the Renaissance, the consensus unraveled slowly but with a relentless surge that continues today.

Where once the peasant could look toward the towers of the medieval cathedral, embodying sacred authority, or the castle expressing secular authority, now the powers of miter and mace are exhausted, replaced by the authority of the state and populist ideologies, fads and fevers—all of which are haunted by a mythological vacuum. The beatific vision is converted to an early retirement on the Sun Coast, the Madonna of Chartres is replaced by the Madonna of MTV, and salvation is found through Halcion, angel dust and the form of crack cocaine called Ecstasy.

If the purpose of myth is to connect us to the four orders of mystery, and if what we have available to our culture is simply one or another ideology—specifically materialism, hedonism or narcissism—then the experience of modernism is the anguish of yearning from within our estrangement. If these ideologies worked for us, we would observe people living the symbolic drama of which Jung spoke. Instead we see the sundry pathologies of a society that has lost mythic community, and the private neuroses of individuals who are indentured to ideologies no longer consonant with the desires and character of their souls.

Several great changes have occurred since the consensus dramatized by Dante, changes that now define the character of modernism.

The first and most obvious change is the movement from the land to the city, from the work of hands to the work of technology, from participation in the great rhythms of nature to the artifices of culture. In this trade-off we have gained an enormous capacity to manipulate matter, to shape our environment, and few of us are nostalgic enough to wish to go back to living off the land. But we have also severed a connection with our own mythic roots as a result. We are, in our controlled environments, disconnected from the Great Mother, "nor can foot feel, being shod," as Gerard Manley Hopkins put it.[12]

Through our ingenuity we have made things of great power, and now we serve those things. The conveniences of the automobile and the computer quickly come to mind, but each exacts a price of alienation from nature and demands fealty to artificial values. This is a huge price, for at bottom we *are* nature and the veneer of civilization is very thin.

Our ancestors lived in an animistic world where soul was in all things. We still knock on wood to summon the assistance of the tutelary spirit there, but we consider such behavior a harmless affectation. The movement from animistic cultures to those theologically based removed people from close contact with the Great Mother and progressively transferred the sacred power in nature to human institutions with divine claims. Thus the post-Dante movement from sacrosanct institutions to the secular state leaves moderns thrice removed from the rhythms of the natural world. This devolution, while providing greater creature comforts, has severed vital linkages between humans and their mysteries. For the comforts of modern civilization, a great ransom has been paid in disconnection and existential angst. As James Hillman has wryly noted,

> The only one God left that is truly universal, omnipresent, omnipotent, observed faithfully in thought and action, joining all human kind in daily acts of devotion: The Economy. That's the God we nourish with actual human blood.[13]

Concomitant with the desacralization of nature and the secularization of culture is the inevitable erosion of myth-consciousness. Perhaps there is no greater testimony to the collapse of mythic connection than the death of God. When we offer such an assertion, we are not making a metaphysical judgment, for whether there is or is not such a metaphysical reality is, by definition, a mystery beyond human comprehension and lies therefore in the province of personal experience and faith. But as a cultural observation, the death of God means that the mythic center that held culture together has lost its power.

---

[12] "God's Grandeur," line 8.
[13] "Once More into the Fray," p. 16.

We may therefore speak of the death of God in a number of ways. The cultural death of God occurs when the mystery is subsumed by cultural values, confused with, for example, nationalism or racism, or misused in the ratification of the powers of the establishment. On such occasions the vital force implied by the word God has left the image and only an icon remains. As the Danish theologian Kierkegaard remarked over a century ago, "The God which can be pointed out is an idol, and the religiosity that makes an outward show is an imperfect form of religiosity."[14]

The philosophical death of God is experienced through the loss of a central hypothesis to which great numbers can lend their volitional, affective assent, that is, feel something to be both true and central for them. The psychological experience of the death of God is recast millions of times in the lives of individuals who feel no vital contact with the numinous, no matter how desperate their yearning nor faithful their attendance at a putative religious institution. Despite the anxious insistence of consciousness, the critical test is whether a person is linked to mystery and is somehow transformed by it. Anything short of that represents the ego's capacity to deceive itself.

The death of the old image, the erosion of the power of once sacred authority, was of course proclaimed *extra ecclesiam* by Nietzsche's mad prophet Zarathustra, by the impact of Darwin and other scientists, but also from within the ranks. Nineteenth-century Biblical scholarship—Strauss's *Das Leben Jesu* (1835), Renan's *La Vie de Jesu* (1863), Hennells's *Inquiry Concerning the Origins of Christianity* (1838) and Feuerbach's *Das Wesens des Christentums* (1855)—demythologized the origins of Western religion. It sought on the one hand to find the human named Jesus, and on the other hand to expose the contamination of the mythologem of the Christ by cultural anthropomorphism and psychological projections.

Where this sincere scholarship left thinking moderns was nowhere clearer than in the plaintive testimony of the art critic John Ruskin: "If only the geologists would let me alone, I could do very well, but those dreadful hammers. I hear the clink of them at the end of every biblical cadence."[15]

---

[14] *Concluding Unscientific Postscript*, p. 142.

[15] See Basil Willey, *Nineteenth Century Studies: Coleridge to Matthew Arnold,* p. 87.

The novelist George Eliot, walking in the gardens at Cambridge, noted that three great ideas have animated culture—God, immortality and duty. The first two she found inconceivable but the third necessary and imperative.[16] How was one to live morally, responsibly in a civilization that had lost its mythic center and eschatological promise?

`The project of the modern artist arose out George Eliot's dilemma. How is one to live when, in the familiar 1917 words of Yeats, "things fall apart," when "the center cannot hold," when "mere anarchy is loosed upon the world"?[17] With the erosion of the mythic center and the concomitant hierarchy of values, nobility, redemption, even tragedy, are impossible. Thus the face of the modern was perhaps best epitomized by Chaplin's Little Tramp and the two tramps of Samuel Beckett who wait by the road for Godot. Who is the little tramp but the modern, whose victimization is so horrendous that we must laugh to release the unbearable tension, and who is Godot but the One the tramps know will never come? It is a long but traceable journey from the high tragedy of Sophocles, even Shakespeare with his bawdy peasants, to the absurdist dramas of Beckett, Pinter, Stoppard and their contemporaries.

It is not too great a leap to suggest that the focal point of pain and yearning, of mystery and madness, is better sought in our time in the explorations of the artists and in the dreams and symptoms of individuals than in the forms and institutions of history. Jung asked where the gods went when they left Olympus; he replied that they went into the solar plexus. When Westerners fell off the roof of the medieval cathedral, he wrote in a letter, they fell into the abyss of the Self.[18] In his essay "Poetry, Myth, and Reality," Philip Wheelwright succinctly expresses the modernist dilemma:

> Our current motivating ideas are not myths but ideologies, lacking transcendental significance. This loss of myth-consciousness is the bond that unites men both with one another and with the unplumbed Mystery from which mankind is sprung and without reference to which the radical significance of things goes to pot. Now a world bereft of radical significance is

---

[16] Ibid., p. 96.
[17] "The Second Coming," in *Collected Poems*, pp. 184-185.
[18] Letter to Olga Fröbe-Kapteyn, *Letters*, vol. 2, p. 569.

not long tolerated; it leaves men radically unstable, so that they will seize at any myth or pseudo-myth that is offered.[19]

Ours is a mythically unstable age, and we an unstable people. If we were born to another time and place, our lives would be, as Thomas Hobbes observed, "nasty, brutish, and short."[20] But chances are we would also have experienced the great connections, the healing and helpful rites, and the clarified norms of behavior.

We were not so born, and to be modern is not just to be alive in this era but to understand what most characterizes our Zeitgeist, namely the erosion of that invisible plane which supports life on the visible plane. The crises of the world are not just "out there" in the geopolitical sphere but "in here," in the individual soul. The questions, explanations and great rhythms that once guided the soul by way of living myth are still within us, still guiding our lives. And we are obliged to render this process more conscious lest we live blindly, false to ourselves and false to nature. To paraphrase the way William Blake put it two centuries ago, we must more consciously create our own myth or be enslaved to the myth of another.[21]

The Modern Sensibility

There are so many facets of the modern experience that one could never begin to address let alone identify them all. I have selected five authors whose works dramatize what it means to live in our time: Goethe, Dostoyevsky, Conrad, Kafka and Camus. Each has illuminated a characteristic aspect of the experience of living in the in-betweenness of the gods. Each incarnates a mythopoeic vision of life.

Historically myth springs autonomously from the deep unconscious, or out of a phenomenological encounter with transcendent personal or tribal experience. As Jung observed:

> The primitive mentality does not *invent* myths, it *experiences* them. Myths are original revelations of the preconscious psyche. . . . Many of these unconscious processes may be indirectly occasioned by conscious-

---

[19] *The Burning Fountain: A Study in the Language of Symbolism,* p. 96.
[20] *Selections,* p. 106.
[21] "I must Create a System or be enslav'd by another Man's"—cited in Northrup Frye, *Fearful Symmetry: A Study of William Blake,* p. 12..

ness, but never by conscious choice. Others appear to arise spontaneously, that is to say, from no discernible or demonstrable conscious cause.[22]

But when the artist necessarily evokes the unconscious in the act of addressing a theme, the deep patterns form and animate the materials in ways that are outside conscious control. For this reason artists from the ancient world to the present have testified to experiencing their intentionality overruled by the emergence of powerful images that seem to come from another place, an experience they have variously described as "possession" by a daimon, the muse or simply inspiration (literally the breath of the divine which blows through the sensibility of the artist). From this experience myth is made.

Thus the artist is often the carrier of the mythological project, the one who, from the intersection of conscious intent and unconscious patterning, makes the myth of the age—mythopoesis. If we are, in Karl Jasper's phrase, to "read the ciphers" of our time,[23] to decipher the mythic texture that lies just beneath the surface, we are obliged to attend the artistic voices around us.

How Faust Became "Faustian"

The historical Faust was born around 1480. He was a lecturer, an alchemist and a threat to conventional Christian beliefs and authorities. When confronted by a Franciscan monk to abjure his ways, Faust reportedly replied that he had pledged his soul to the Devil in return for the knowledge of the darker powers. His resolute defiance of the Church sparked the interest of many, if only to condemn his heresy.

The first text about Faust was written in 1587 by a Lutheran minister, Johann Spies. Naturally, Faust was condemned for his blasphemy and served as an exemplum of the damned soul. Many other texts appeared with different slants on the story, but all with the moral judgment paramount. Shakespeare's contemporary, Christopher Marlowe, portrayed him as an heroic figure in *The Tragical History of Dr. Faustus,* but damned just the same. The Chorus's final pronouncement is clear:

---

[22] "The Psychology of the Child Archetype," *The Archetypes and the Collective Unconscious,* CW 9i, par. 261.

[23] *Philosophy and the World,* p. 8.

Faustus is gone; regard his hellish fall,
Whose fiendful torture may exhort the wise
Only to wonder at unlawful things,
Whose deepness doth entice such forward wits
To practice more than heavenly power permits.[24]

Marlowe's take on what had quickly become a Faust legend, and an archetypal encounter between good and evil and the imperiled human soul, was more Greek than Christian. Marlowe was less interested in the fact that Faust had transgressed Christian theological boundaries than that he had committed the sin of hubris. Hubris is the failure to recognize the distinction between what is human and what divine, between what is permitted to human consciousness and what remains the proper province of the gods. Hubris may arise either from flawed judgment or from inflated vanity that arrogates to itself capacities it does not possess; in either case there are deleterious consequences. Marlowe's reading of the Faust mythologem anticipates Goethe's more than do the various diatribes against Faust from evangelical sources.

Faust was a life-long preoccupation of the man whom many call the German Shakespeare, Johann Wolfgang von Goethe. He started work on his *Faust* in 1773, published Part One in 1808, and was still revising Part Two a few months before his death in 1832. One may argue that the spirit of the modern begins with certain classical Greek ideas, such as the attempt of the pre-Socratics to find a nontheological metaphysics, the articulation of the scientific method by Bacon, the mind-body split of Descartes in the seventeenth century, or the recognition by Kant of a priori categories of mind as the constitutive nature of nature in the late eighteenth century. But to my mind the essential characteristic of modernism is first embodied in Goethe's take on the Faust legend.

Goethe's Faust is less hubristic and damned, more a paradigm of human yearning to know all, to live with a reckless passion for truth and to step out into the empty space of the time between the gods. One gets the clear sense in reading *Faust* that God and Satan are more the celestial machinery on which to hang the spiritual journey of Faust than the normative, metaphysical powers of the Christian tradition.

---

[24] Cited by Walter Kaufmann in Goethe, *Faust,* p. 16.

If we could say of the classical Greek sensibility, as depicted by Sophocles for example, that the highest good was the restoration of the proper balance between hubristic humans and capricious gods, and that for the medieval, Christian mythos, as depicted by Dante for example, the highest value was salvation, then we could say that the highest goal for Goethe, and the modernist era, was self-realization.

In the Prologue, Mephistopheles describes Faust to the Lord, saying that while Faust's "spirit's ferment drives him far," and he "half knows how foolish is his quest," yet

> From heaven he demands the fairest star,
> And from the earth all joys that he thinks best;
> and all that's near and all that's far
> cannot soothe the upheaval in his breast.[25]

Later Faust concludes, *"Dasein ist Pflicht, und wars ein Augenblick,"* which may be translated, "Total realization is imperative, if only for a moment," or "Existence is a duty, even for only a moment."[26]

Faust embodies Goethe's agreement with his contemporary Lessing's famous aphorism that if God had two hands, one representing the truth and the other the search for truth, one must choose the latter.[27] He anticipates Thomas Mann's Hans Castorp who says, "It is more moral to lose oneself and even abandon oneself to perdition than to preserve oneself."[28] Or one thinks of T. S. Eliot's essay on Charles Baudelaire, wherein he writes that one may pray for the redemption of the infidel Baudelaire, but at least he had the spiritual depth to earn damnation, rather than what the anti-Nazi martyr Dietrich Bonhoeffer would later call "cheap grace."[29]

Faust's personality seems familiar to us for he embodies a restlessness, a deep sea-surge within. At the play's beginning he is suffering a suicidal depression. Having learned all that he can know in the disciplines of his medieval setting—philosophy, jurisprudence, medicine and theology—he has reached the end of those four piers where the great ocean roars and

---

[25] Ibid., lines 302-307.
[26] Ibid., line 1552.
[27] *Lessing's Theological Writings*, p. 248.
[28] *The Magic Mountain*, p. 52.
[29] *Letters and Papers from Prison*, p. 112.

beckons still. Yet, he laments, "for all our science and art / we can know nothing."[30]

He nears the precipice of suicide, half out of despair, half yearning for the abyss. His sensibility is typically modern, a consuming passion for totality, for wholeness. Some have sought it in love, some in drugs, some in religion, but all of us still resonate to his dilemma: "Though I know much, I should like to know all."[31] He knows, as we do, that "two souls, alas, are dwelling in my breast,"[32] one clinging to this earth in passionate embrace and one longing, in the words of Gustave Flaubert, "to make music that would melt the stars."[33]

The Mephistopheles who offers Faust his opportunity for transcendence is not the Devil of old in red underwear with horns and pitchfork. This character comes in the modality most likely to touch Faust—as an itinerant scholar. At first, Faust is also inclined to associate him with his traditional attributes, as Liar, Lord of the Flies, but Mephistopheles quickly corrects him. He is not the simple opposite of the good but rather "part of the force which would / do evil evermore, and yet creates the good."[34] He is "part of the darkness which gave birth to light."[35] Thus, Mephistopheles embodies what Jung called the archetype of the shadow.

The shadow represents that which is excluded from consciousness because it is threatening, painful, embarrassing or destabilizing. The shadow may be experienced individually or collectively; it represents a wider, richer range of energy that often operates autonomously and invades conscious life in disturbing ways, but which is ultimately necessary for the expansion and completion of consciousness. The shadow has too often been split off in Western thinking and we know, psychologically, that whatever is split off reinsinuates itself through behavioral eruptions or projections onto others. Jung explored the psychological consequences of this split in "Answer to Job," and the recent lesson of the Holocaust is an in-

---

[30] Goethe, *Faust,* lines 363-364.
[31] Ibid., line 601.
[32] Ibid., line 1112.
[33] *Madame Bovary,* p. 206.
[34] Goethe, *Faust,* linee 1336-1337.
[35] Ibid., line 1350.

escapable reminder of what one's own darkness can do when projected onto others.

Thus Mephistopheles for Goethe is an inherent part of the totality, the denial of which, even by the high-minded scholar, leads him to destroy a simple soul, the maiden Gretchen, through his unconsciousness.

When Mephistopheles takes Faust to the Witch's Kitchen, the head Witch also misunderstands the more variegated richness of this modern version and welcomes him as "Squire Satan." To which Mephistopheles replies,"That name is out, hag!" Why?—

> It's dated, called a fable; men are clever,
> but they are just as badly off as ever:
> the Evil One is gone, the evil ones remain.[36]

With that last sentence, the modernist mythos begins. The Evil One, with capital letters, represents the traditional hierarchy of values, the common mythos operative up to Dante but with less and less authority ever since. The Evil One as a necessary hypothesis stands on a par no doubt with the Good One. If the name and concomitant authority of the former is no more, what then of the latter? The insistence of Mephistopheles that the old authority behind such names is gone sets the stage for the modernist experience of the wasteland, the space between words, and the anguish of waiting for Godot.

On the other hand, and here's the rub, the evil ones remain. When Hannah Arendt went to Jerusalem to report on the trial and subsequent execution of Adolf Eichmann, she half expected to see a tail protruding from the man who had said he would go to his grave laughing because he knew six million Jews had preceded him. What she saw was a balding, bespectacled nondescript who had passed unnoticed for decades in Buenos Aires. Eichmann was the epitome of the demythologization of modernism. As much as we might wish to demonize Hitler, to blame the Devil, the truth is that millions of ordinary citizens projected their own shadow onto him. In turn, he activated in them the pagan energies that lay just beneath the veneer of thousands of years of civilization.

To describe Eichmann and the required collusion of millions, Arendt

---

[36] Ibid., lines 2504-2509.

coined the phrase, "the banality of evil."[37] No devils in red underwear; only sober citizens intent on living in their unconscious ways. And no cultural instrumentality we had invented—theology, science, humanism—was sufficient to resist the seduction of the shadow. As George Steiner pointed out, "We know that some of the men who devised and administered Auschwitz had been taught to read Shakespeare and Goethe, and continued to do so."[38]

Arendt's reminder that the evil ones remain, that they are us, that the shadow is our own, is as much anticipated by Goethe's Mephistopheles as the thought is still denied by many even today. It takes no guy with horns lurking about to create darkness; we carry so much of it with us all the time. For all the nobility of his yearning, Faust is a person who will also bring sadness and destruction in his wake. The magnificent accomplishments of modernism are tempered by the accompanying shadow. As Jung once noted, the greater the light, the darker the shadow. And Goethe, the sage of Weimar, who helped dramatize the shadow, allegedly spoke as his dying words, "More light!"[39]

In addition to Goethe's dramatization of Faust as the prototype of human aspiration, of the yearning for eternity, and as the new being seeking light and finding dark in a time between the gods, there is a third element to the Faust imago which typifies the modern experience: Faust clearly takes on the burden of his own salvation.

If the old metaphysical powers are dead, and if we walk carrying as much darkness as light, then we are now obliged to stand more consciously and responsibly before the universe. In Jungian terms, each of us has become responsible for our own individuation. Individuation is not only the inherent, natural impulse within to become what we were meant to be, but the moral imperative of consciousness to cooperate, to further

---

[37] *Eichmann in Jerusalem,* p. 81. Or, as Thomas Merton reflected: "The sanity of Eichmann is disturbing . . . . We can no longer assume that because a man is 'sane' he is therefore in his 'right mind.' The whole concept of sanity in a society where spiritual values have lost their meaning is itself meaningless." ("A Devout Meditation in Memory of Adolf Eichmann," cited in Jim Forest, *Living with Wisdom,* p. 133)

[38] *Language and Silence: Essays on Language, Literature and the Inhuman,* p. 5.

[39] *The Oxford Dictionary of Quotations,* p. 230.

the mysterious ends of nature through the particularities of the individual.

All of nature depends on the development of the individual, from the gnat to the giraffe, from the mole to the mammal. This is a sacred summons, but with or without a metaphysical backdrop of sureties, we are obliged to take responsibility for the meaning of our lives. We are obliged to ask, as Jung did, whether we are we related to something infinite or not.[40] However we answer, we are nonetheless burdened with the responsibility of creating meaning in our lives. We are condemned to freedom, though the whiff of existential angst is enough to blow many off course, back to some safe ideological haven.

Goethe's Faust stepped boldly into that empty place between the gods. "Of the beyond I have no thought . . . my joys come from this earth," he tells Mephistopheles, who would impress him with intimations of immortality.[41] Faust wagers his soul. In effect, he bets Mephistopheles that the depth and yearning of the human soul is so great that no magical mystery tour, no temple of delights, no sundry seductions of soma, will suffice to surfeit it. "If ever I recline, calmed on a bed of sloth, / You may destroy me then and there,"[42] for "as I grow stagnant I shall be a slave, / whether or not to anyone indebted."[43] Thus the heroic challenge, debate perhaps, between them.

Faust wagers his soul's worth and depth, takes responsibility for its salvation, and clearly notes that it is the journey of the soul, not its resting place, that constitutes the meaning. His salvation lies not in some Valhalla, nor his damnation in some dreadful Dis, but in the daily living of the high adventure, between worlds, between stars and earth, between gods.

In sum, Goethe's mythopoeic rendering of the Faust imago launches the modern era because of these three features which are so indisputably features of our psychology: the urgent need to explore all avenues, no matter how risky; the shifting of the moral burden from an external hierarchy of values and institutional referents; and the assumption of the personal burden of salvation or individuation.

---

[40] *Memories, Dreams, Reflections,* p. 325.

[41] Goethe, *Faust,* lines 1660, 1664.

[42] Ibid., lines 1692-1693.

[43] Ibid., lines 1710-1711.

We can no longer adopt the easy optimism of the last century that our Faustian urge to know all would bring about a golden age. The same tree under which the sage of Weimar once sat to write *Faust*, later was protected and served as the center point of *K-Z Lager Buchenwald*. Karl Shapiro, in "The Progress of Faust," uses the ambiguities of the word progress, both in the sense of procession and as advancement. He traces the history of the Faust imago and cites its most recent manifestation:

> Five years unknown to enemy and friend
> He hid, appearing on the sixth to pose
> In an American desert at war's end
> Where, at his back, a dome of atoms rose.[44]

We can, and will, explore all avenues, from the intricacies of atoms and genes to the amplitudes of outer space, but we can no longer naively claim the powers once the property of the gods without also taking on their burdens. Like Phaeton of ancient Greek myth, we careen about on the chariot of the sun, but without a metaphysical framework by which to understand and chart our course. In the words of Wallace Stevens, we are "unsponsored, free . . . inescapable."[45]

Thus in isolation comes the great adventure. As Faust asserts to Mephistopheles, if my soul is easily diverted from this high adventure, I am already dead and you can have me. Faust then places himself in the paradox Nietzsche described when he said we are both the abyss and the tightrope across the abyss.[46] We are the open emptiness, to be filled by courage and by choice, and we are the fragile thread by which to traverse the abysmal terrors.

Thus Faust is the first modern, full of yearning, which in its excesses becomes "Faustian." Stepping free of metaphysical supports or constraints, he becomes responsible for his soul's meaning. His example, his dignity and suffering, and his dilemma, are ours to answer in our own way. Goethe intuitively sensed and artistically described the falling away of the old mythos and the obligation of the modern to live more consciously in the great in-between.

---

[44] Richard Ellman and Robert O'Clair, eds., *Modern Poems*, p. 263.
[45] "Sunday Morning," in ibid., p. 94.
[46] "Thus Spake Zarathustra," in *The Portable Nietzsche*, p. 126.

The underground man

In 1851, just outside of London, the first truly international exhibition of trade and culture opened in a glass and steel structure called the Crystal Palace. The nations of the world gathered their new machines, their products and their pride to display the ways in which they had bent nature to serve their will.

Explicitly their proclamations trumpeted the cult of progress and the optimistic doctrine of meliorism, the view that with the Promethean powers of education, technology and material wealth, a new age was dawning in which the ancient scourges of disease, poverty, exploitation and war would be eradicated. Implicitly, they represented the youthful ego-flush of the Faustian complex.

Sixty-five years later, 60,000 British youth would be slaughtered in the first twenty-four hours of the Battle of the Somme. Eighty-nine years later the Luftwaffe would use the shell of the Crystal Palace as a navigational checkpoint as they began their bombing runs on London in the Battle of Britain. Ninety-four years later the Western powers would enter Babi Yar, Bergen-Belsen, Mauthausen, Oranienburg, Dachau, Sobibor, Sachsenhausen, Treblinka, Terezienstadt, Ravensbrück and Auschwitz. So much for meliorism.

While few today would cavil at the great achievements of modern civilization, the giddy optimism of our great-grandparents wears thin at such a litany of railroad crossings and scenic spots located just outside the clusters of cities and just off the Autobahn. One man, who surely must have seemed mad to his contemporaries, foresaw such a future, for he had seen more deeply into the soul than his contemporaries. What he saw was too disturbing for them to acknowledge, but historical events have obligated us to look and agree. That man was Fyodor Dostoyevsky.

In *Notes from Underground*, written in 1864, Dostoyevsky surveyed the Crystal Palace which had so enchanted his culture and concluded:

> Men love abstract reasoning and neat systemization so much that they think nothing of distorting the truth, closing their eyes and ears to contrary evidence to preserve their logical constructions. . . . What is it in us that is mellowed by civilization? All it does, I'd say, is to develop in man a capacity to feel a greater variety of sensations. And nothing, absolutely noth-

ing else. And through this development, man will yet learn how to enjoy bloodshed.[47]

Dostoyevsky's self-portrait was perhaps the first truly psychological view of humankind. This is not to say that one could not find profound psychological insights scattered throughout literary and religious texts, but perhaps in no single volume can one find a more probing psychological portrait than in *Notes from Underground.* We must remember that Dostoyevsky was writing before Freud and the discoveries of depth psychology. Freud's first significant book was *Studies in Hysteria* in 1895, and his *Interpretation of Dreams* came out only at the beginning of this century.

Indeed, one of the consequences of that erosion of traditional myth which we have observed was a major paradigm shift. Since Faust it has become increasingly necessary to define and describe human beings in their social setting rather than their theological context. The Age of Sophocles and the Age of Dante were understood *sub specie eternitatus.* But the Age of Angst, as *Time* once characterized it on a cover, is more commonly defined by class, nation, gender, economic status and neurosis. In fact, all the disciplines we call the social sciences—economics, political science, sociology, urban studies, anthropology and psychology—originated in the nineteenth century and derive from this massive paradigm shift. Jung once observed that psychology was the newest of the so-called sciences because the insights it embodies used to be carried by the great myths and religions.[48]

Freud noted that humankind has gone through three major relocations in the cosmos, three dethronements of ego inflation: the work of Copernicus taught us that we were not the center of the universe as Ptolemy had depicted; Darwin taught us that we were animals after all and not necessarily the evolutionary apex; and depth psychology weighed in with the unsettling notion that most of the time we paragons of consciousness are controlled by unconscious drives.

Dostoyevsky's underground man is a metaphor for the life that thrives beneath consciousness, life which seethes and disrupts the well-laid plans

---

[47] *Notes from Underground,* pp. 107-108.
[48] "The Spiritual Problem of Modern Man," *Civilization in Transition,* CW 10, pars. 159ff.

of meliorism and self-congratulation. His portrait of humanity is often repugnant to consciousness, to self-esteem and to ego inflation, but it is indisputably honest, accurate and compelling.

There are four psychological insights in *Notes from Underground* that to my mind are quintessentially modern: our inherent narcissism, our will to chaos and self-destruction, our perversions, and our compulsion for radical self-assertion.

No work of Western thought begins with less mellifluous words than *Notes from Underground:*

> I am a sick man . . . a mean man. There's nothing attractive about me. I think there's something wrong with my liver. But, actually I don't understand a damn thing about my sickness; I'm not even too sure what it is that's ailing me. . . . Now then, what does a decent man like to talk about most? Himself, of course. So I'll talk about myself.[49]

The underground man is unredeemably self-preoccupied. Given the context of Victorian literature he is a rare bird indeed. Instead of one who carries the traditional heroic values, he is the first of a type who became quite common in modern literature—the anti-hero. An entire genre was launched by this character who refuses to put himself in a positive light, refuses to fight for the old capital letters (Truth, Beauty, Goodness, Country, God). His type is modern because modern psychology, if not modern history, has forced us to accept that the narcissistic, infantile id furtively works its will beneath the nose of the haughty superego and undermines the ego's efforts to pull off a respectable compromise.

The underground man confesses what we fear might be true about ourselves: "I was always guilty in the first place, and what is most vexing is that I was guilty without guilt, by virtue of the laws of nature."[50] His narcissism is insufferable. He even has raised the exquisite suffering of a toothache to a high art: "It's this moaning that expresses the pleasure of the sufferer, for if he didn't enjoy it, he wouldn't moan."[51]

But his self-preoccupation not only adumbrates the leitmotif of our current age, it also digs deeply below the veneer of Victorian pieties to an

---

[49] *Notes from Underground,* pp. 90, 93.
[50] Ibid., p. 95.
[51] Ibid., p. 100.

honest confrontation with the shadow:

> To you, I'm no longer the hero I tried to appear at first, but simply a despicable little man. So be it. I'm glad you've managed to see through me. . . . After all, how can a man with my lucidity of perception respect himself?[52]

By the time we reach midlife we surely have learned the truth of Mark Twain's aphorism, "Man is the only animal that blushes, and has reason to."[53] Whoever has not gained a significant measure of self-loathing has not become very conscious. Thus the underground man, having espied an officer of the cavalry striding ostentatiously and brandishing his saber, muses about himself:

> This kind of showing off is just as much in poor taste as the sabre rattling of that officer I mentioned. But I ask you, who on earth goes around showing off his sickness, and even glorying in it? On second thought though, I'd say that everyone does. People do pride themselves on their infirmities and I, probably, more than anyone.[54]

What an extraordinary insight, and yet so inescapably true, as is clear from the posturing of politicians, the bluster of generals, the inanities of sitcoms, the eschatological claims of commercials, or one's own behavior as recently as yesterday. Any therapist sees how a client clings to neurosis, loves the symptoms, the hiding-out place of blame or same-old, same-old, rather than risk the trauma of change. As W. H. Auden noted:

> We would rather be ruined than changed,
> We would rather die in our dread
> Than climb the cross of the moment
> And let our illusions die.[55]

The underground man is especially irritated by what philosophers have called the Socratic fallacy. Plato argued, through his persona Socrates, that humans will not commit evil acts if they truly understand them to be evil. When they do evil, it is because they do not truly understand the good,

---

[52] Ibid., p. 101.

[53] *Oxford Dictionary of Quotations,* p. 554.

[54] *Notes from Underground,* p. 93.

[55] "The Age of Anxiety," in *Collected Poems,* p. 407.

and it is the good (the Good) that animates the soul. What does the underground man have to say about this moral and historical optimism?—

> Oh, the innocence of it! . . . What about the millions of facts that show that men, deliberately and in full knowledge of what their real interests were, spurned them and rushed in a different direction? . . . Doesn't this suggest that stubbornness and willfulness were stronger in these people than their interests?[56]

Dostoyevsky's contemporary, Nietzsche, was mining a similar vein when, in his safe position as professor of linguistics at the provincial University of Basel, he overthrew the world. Not only was God dead—that is, the reified icon of the institutional Church no longer carried numinosity—but the future had fallen into the hands of the Overman and his "will to power."[57] It is one of the supreme ironies of history that the Nazis took this iconoclast and made him a part of their pseudo-intellectual iconography, took his will to power and identified it with the *Wehrmacht,* took his deep love of the individual and made him the emotional source of collective identification in the raised salute to Fascism.

Nietzsche's will to power echoes Dostoyevsky's will to destruction, will to chaos. While the avatars of convention may tremble, this will is what defines the individual even as it threatens society. This rogue may ultimately be what saves humans from those other parts of themselves that operate autonomously, those Quislings of the psyche that sell out for security. Both of these prophets were speaking out of a deep source and affirming the self-destructive but ineluctable will of the individual.

The vision articulated by Nietzsche and Dostoyevsky was perverse but not perverted, and it was perverse only because it was counter to the prevailing collective values. Both, of course, were celebrants of the perverted (from *per,* away, and *vertere,* to turn) because they "turned away from," and thus earned the condemnation, the opprobrium, of the mass. But each was true to a new vision of and appreciation for the individual. And who is to say what is the true path? The group? In their identification of the indi-

---

[56] *Notes from Underground,* pp. 105-106.
[57] "Thus Spake Zarathustra," in *The Portable Nietzsche,* p. 226. (Nietzsche's reading of the soul currents of our time is haunting: "Don't you smell the slaughterhouses and ovens of the spirit even now?" Ibid., p. 288)

vidual as perverted and yet the only available source of renewal, they celebrated, in an underground way, the delicious paradox that such a confluence embodies.

In the midst of an activist social clime dead set on building bigger and
thereforer better, a culture based on the primacy of rational thought, the
underground man dares to suggest:

> And what would the natural, illogical fruit of heightened consciousness be
> if not inertia, by which I mean consciously sitting with folded arms! . . .
> Spontaneous people and men of action can act precisely because they are
> limited and stupid.[58]

> And so, in the end, ladies and gentlemen, it's best to do nothing at all!
> Conscious inertia is the best![59]

His parody extends to the reductio ad absurdum:

> I couldn't even conceive of being second best; that's why, in real life, I re-
> signed myself so easily to being last . . . a hero couldn't be altogether de-
> filed by mud, so why not wallow in it?[60]

St. Paul confessed that although he knew the good, for reasons outside
of conscious control he did not do the good. Likewise, underneath Dostoyevsky's caricature pulses a profound respect for the nonrational life
force While he could not know of the horrors of collectivization, the Stal-
inist purges and gulags, he correctly read the signs. He saw that the price
of the Crystal Palace would be paid by the progressive loss of individual-
ity. His fear of the danger of group-think anticipates George Orwell's
1984 and "Politics and the English Language."

"I admit that reason is a good thing," asserts the underground man—

> No argument about that. But reason is only reason, and it only satisfies
> man's rational requirements. Desire, on the other hand, is the manifesta-
> tion of life . . . and it encompasses everything from reason down to
> scratching oneself. And although, when we're guided by our desires, life
> may often turn into a messy affair, it's still life and not a series of extrac-
> tions of square roots.[61]

---

[58] Ibid., p. 102.
[59] Ibid., p. 120.
[60] Ibid., p. 136.
[61] Ibid., p. 112.

It is this irrational desire, this life force which gets messy at times, that carries the seed of the individual.

A man can wish upon himself . . . something harmful, stupid, and even completely idiotic. He will do it in order to establish his right to wish for the most idiotic things and not to be obliged to have only sensible wishes.[62]

The underground man represents what we most deeply are and his perverse opinions represent our deepest freedom. Indeed, our meaning comes, he feels, not by participation in the collective, but in the daily anarchy of desire. He concludes:

It seems to me that the meaning of man's life consists in proving to himself every minute that he's a man and not a piano key. And man will keep proving it and paying for it with his own skin; he will turn into a troglodyte if need be. . . . I cannot help rejoicing that things are still the way they are and that, for the time being, nobody knows worth a damn what determines our desires.[63]

Ask yourself whose anthropology has proved more prophetic of the twentieth century—that of the apostles of progress, the meliorists, or that of the perverse seer, the underground man? In his articulation of our reflexive narcissism, our will to self-destruction, our sundry perversities and our irrational assertion of self, the underground man offers a more disturbing albeit more accurate dramatization of the modern sensibility. He even celebrates suffering as the necessary precondition of consciousness. The new Age of Progress will presumably alleviate suffering but that could also bring about a diminution of individual awareness. In the face of the calculus of collectivity the underground man asserts:

Consciousness . . . is of a much higher order than twice two. . . . With consciousness we have nothing much to do . . . but we can at least lacerate ourselves from time to time, which does liven us up a bit. It may go against progress, but it's better than nothing.[64]

Dostoyevsky insists on the heuristic value of suffering and the raw edges of individual desire, perversity and assertiveness. Against T.S.

---

[62] Ibid.
[63] Ibid., p. 115.
[64] Ibid., p. 118.

Eliot's wasteland and hollow men, the banality of Eichmann and Beckett's tramps, the anonymity of group-think, he sides with the medieval aphorism that suffering is the fastest horse to completion, and Jung's conclusion that "neurosis is suffering which has not yet found its meaning."[65] Against the engineered society embodied in the metaphor of the Crystal Palace he expresses his rebellion: "I'm afraid of such a palace precisely because it's indestructible and because I won't ever be allowed to stick my tongue out at it."[66]

In the radical metaphor of the underground man, Dostoyevsky obliges moderns to see themselves as they really are, not as they pretend to be. It was this man, operating *sub rosa* in the rag-and-bone shop of the heart, who created modern history, not the architects of steel and glass palaces.

In the heart of darkness

In an 1898 novella of less than eighty pages, Joseph Conrad furthers Dostoyevsky's anthropology. In 1876 King Leopold of Belgium gathered the nations of Europe to Brussels for a conference whose purpose was to carve up someone else's land. But such an ignoble thought must be draped to conceal its sinister form, so the conference was called "to open to civilization the only part of our globe where Christianity has not penetrated and to pierce the darkness which envelops the entire population."[67] Old Europe, perfecter of pogroms, auto-da-fés, and soon the concentration camp, was willing to share the benefits of its culture with its lesser brethren, especially those brethren living near ivory and mineral deposits.

The protagonist of Conrad's novella, Marlow, undertakes a voyage to the interior to gain intelligence about one Kurtz, a station master who has gone before him. Marlow's reflections along the way make clear that we are asked to look beyond the imperialist pieties to see the rotten core:

> The conquest of the earth, which mostly means the taking it away from those who have a different complexion or slightly flatter noses than ourselves, is not a pretty thing when you look into it too much. What redeems it is the idea only. An idea at the back of it . . . something you can

---

[65] "Psychotherapists or the Clergy," *Psychology and Religion,* CW 11, par. 497.
[66] *Notes from Underground,* p. 118.
[67] Conrad, *The Heart of Darkness,* p. 87.

set up, and bow down before, and offer a sacrifice to.[68]

Such "ideas" are necessary to mobilize millions. Such ideas will make them wage slaves, convince them to invest in artificially generated needs, and even to march off to serve what Wilfred Owen called, "The old Lie: *Dulce et decorum est / Pro patria mori.* "[69] But what moves masses are not ideas really, but ideologies, ideas set up as unquestioned, normative for all, and exclusionary of counter-ideas. Marlow knows what lurks beneath the idea of Christianizing black Africa: "The word 'ivory' rang in the air, was whispered, was sighed. You would think they were praying to it."[70]

Ultimately Marlow finds station chief Kurtz who is now quite mad and lives as a petty potentate in the jungle. Kurtz, who once set off with noble motives, has, as the underground man predicted, been corrupted by what was darkest within him. He is the paradigm of the modern who has no thoughts of his own and believes the thoughts of his culture to be pretty and convincing. Conrad speaks of all of us who have naively wandered into the wilderness:

> The wilderness had found him out early, and had taken a terrible vengeance.
> . . . it had whispered to him things about himself which he did not know,
> things of which he had no conception till he took counsel with the great
> solitude. . . . It echoed loudly within him because he was hollow at the
> core.[71]

While Kurtz is overwhelmed by "the horror" without and "the horror" within,[72] Marlow struggles to balance the opposites. If madness is being possessed by an obsessive thought, a one-sided vision, then sanity is the ability to juggle, to balance the opposites and to find the higher third in every dialectic. Marlow, after all the high drama and high nonsense about "the white man's burden," concludes, "The most you can hope from it is some knowledge of yourself."[73]

It does not seem much to have obtained after such a long journey, but

---

[68] Ibid., p. 7.
[69] Simon Fuller, ed., *The Poetry of War, 1914-1989,* p. 20.
[70] *The Heart of Darkness,* p. 23.
[71] Ibid., p. 59.
[72] Ibid., p. 72.
[73] Ibid., p. 71.

Marlow's achievement is the sine qua non. Without self-knowledge, that is to say, a feeling self-recognition, a moral consciousness, only injury to self or others can result. Setting off to bring light into the dark continent, the moderns carried their darkness with them and made a grand botch of it. With a modicum of moral awareness, they might better have stayed home and confronted their own dark hearts and perhaps have prevented their youth from marching off to die by the millions sixteen years later.

Conrad, like Goethe and Dostoyevsky, obliges us to view humankind through a psychological prism. It is insufficient to understand our time in merely political or economic terms. To understand what it means to be human obliges a growing awareness of the deepest designs of the soul.

Czech mate

W. H. Auden once wrote that Franz Kafka stood in relation to our age as Dante stood to his. High praise indeed. Born in Prague in 1883, before he died at the age of forty-one Kafka wrote many short stories and several novels in a seemingly naturalistic style that belied their essentially parabolic character. Through images he succeeded in objectifying various psychic states common to us all. He depicted the power of the negative parent complex in "The Judgment," the omnipotence of guilt in "The Penal Colony" and *The Trial,* the remoteness of God in *The Castle* and "The Hunter Gracchus," and radical alienation and depersonalization in "Metamorphosis" and "A Report to an Academy."

Kafka worked by day for an insurance company and labored at night over his stories, sharing them with only a few close friends. When he died he asked that they all be destroyed, but his executor, Max Brod, chose to save them and bring Kafka to the rest of the world. His stories seemed as strange to his contemporaries as they sometimes still seem. Even after the underground man, how can we countenance a protagonist who is turned into a cockroach in the midst of his family, or a camp where one is strapped to a machine that etches the words "Honor Thy Superiors" into living flesh?

Yet, less than twenty years after his death, Kafka's family was sent off to Auschwitz for the crime of having been born Jews. They and their co-religionists were called *Einzgesiefer* (vermin) by the S.S. Anyone who forecast such things at the beginning of the century would have been considered crazy. But Kafka, while not a political writer, limned the temper of the time and the mazy motions of the underworld.

Perhaps no story of Kafka's more presciently depicts the modern dilemma than "A Country Doctor," written in the second decade of this century. A rural physician is summoned out in the middle of a snow storm to see a patient in a village. When he arrives the entire population is gathered around a young man who asks the doctor to save him. The physician examines the youth and can find nothing wrong. Save me, save me, he is again asked. This time he sees a huge rose-like wound emanating from the side, clearly a symbolic wound. When the physician announces that he cannot save him, the villagers leap upon the doctor, strip his clothing in a ritual divestiture of his powers, and fling him out into the countryside to try to find his way home. Along the way the doctor muses:

> That is what people are like in my district. Always expecting the impossible from the doctor. They have lost their ancient beliefs; the parson sits at home and unravels his vestments, one after another; but the doctor is supposed to be omnipotent with his merciful surgeon's hands. . . . If they misuse me for sacred ends, I let that happen to me too.[74]

The shift that began just after Dante is completed in Kafka. The shift from ecclesiastical authority to secular has transpired, but the secular authority, the avatars of progress and the Crystal Palace, cannot save either. The Victorians inflated the powers of modern science into scientism, that is, the naive belief in the efficacy of science, but scientism has given way to the skepticism and disillusion of modernism.

The road from Dante to Kafka is direct; each articulated the vision of his age. For the former, one could still appeal to the hierarchy of values implicit in the institutions of mace and miter; the latter wanders a universe of failed institutions. Declares Kafka's Gracchus:

> I am here, more than that I do not know, further than that I cannot go. My ship has no rudder, and it is driven by the wind that blows in the undermost regions of death.[75]

Few artists have more bleakly rendered the modern condition.

---

[74] *Selected Short Stories of Franz Kafka,* pp. 153-154.
[75] "The Hunter Gracchus," ibid., p. 187.

After the Fall

The last author I have chosen to dramatize the dilemma of modernism is Albert Camus. This Algerian-born, Nobel Prize-winning French author died in 1960 at the height of his powers when his car skidded off the road and collided with a tree. He, like Dostoyevsky and Kafka before him, discerned the narcissism, vacuity and isolation of the modern. In his many short stories and the novels *The Plague* and *The Stranger,* Camus depicts the emptiness and shock, the post-traumatic stress, of the aftermath of World War Two and the Cold War. But it is in *The Fall* that he most succinctly depicts modern individuals adrift.

The Fall is set in a bar in Amsterdam, a city whose circular canals remind the protagonist of the circles of Dante's Hell, but this is a "middle-class hell, of course, peopled with bad dreams."[76] The entire text is the monologue of a patron of the bar who tells a story which exists on two levels. On the one hand, his loss of innocence is experienced by the recent devotion to the Idea, the method, the efficiency which Conrad's Marlow saw but which is now perfected by

> our Hitlerian brethren. . . . What a cleanup! Seventy-five thousand Jews deported or assassinated; that's real vacuum-cleaning. I admire that diligence, that methodical patience! When one has no character one has to apply a method.[77]

On the other hand, the loss of connection to the gods, to the great rhythms, leads Camus to conclude, "A single sentence will suffice for modern man: he fornicated and read the papers."[78] He sees the modern as emotionally blunted and narcissistic: "Have you noticed that death alone awakens our feelings?"[79] and "He can't love without self-love."[80] This malaise has eaten into the soul, thus "we lack the energy of evil as well as the energy of good."[81]

The salvationist comforts of past cultures are only nostalgic memories

---

[76] *The Fall,* p. 14.
[77] Ibid., p. 11.
[78] Ibid., p. 6.
[79] Ibid., p. 32.
[80] Ibid., p. 34.
[81] Ibid., p. 83.

for Camus' characters, even if falling snowflakes were to turn into heavenly doves:

> What an invasion! Let's hope they are bringing good news. Everyone will be saved, eh?—and not only the elect. . . . The whole shooting match, eh! Come now, admit that you would be flabbergasted if a chariot came down from heaven to carry me off, or if the snow suddenly caught fire. You don't believe it? Nor do I.[82]

These folk wander in the wasteland of life without mythic connection. They are no longer actors, to use Jung's metaphor, in the symbolic drama.

Most of all, the protagonist is haunted by the memory of a night he crossed a bridge and saw a young woman about to hurl herself into the icy waters. He thought to stop, but he had places to go, people to see. Now, if only he could cross that bridge again and see that young life in peril, then he could say,

> "O young woman, throw yourself into the water again so that I may a second time have the chance of saving both of us." A second time, eh, what a risky suggestion! Just suppose . . . that we should be taken literally? We'd have to go through with it. Brr . . . ! The water's so cold! But let's not worry! It's too late now. It will always be too late. Fortunately![83]

The "fortunately" of Camus is not quite the *felix culpa* of medieval theology. He knows, but his knowledge cannot save him. The institutions can no longer save him; the country doctor cannot save him; his own consciousness cannot save him. His damnation is to be left a prisoner of that same consciousness, to be, in the words of Gerard Manley Hopkins, our own "sweating selves."[84] Camus' characters have lost the heaven out there and are now living the hell in here.

These five authors—Goethe, Dostoyevsky, Conrad, Kafka and Camus —depict an essentially psychological view of life. They do not use, and often did not know, the terms and case studies of contemporary psychology, but they certainly discerned the movement of soul that characterizes modern experience.

---

[82] Ibid., pp. 145-146.

[83] Ibid., p. 147.

[84] "I Wake and Feel the Fell of Dark," *Poems of Gerard Manley Hopkins*, p. 77.

This discussion has been brief, and other worthy examples could have been included, but the works chosen are central to any effort to understand the implicit modern myth in an age lacking explicit myth. They describe the psychic landscape we attempt to understand by reading newspapers, studying history and juggling data of all kinds. But the place from whence those facts arise is a place deep within each of us.

If we are to understand ourselves and our time, we are obliged to adopt this essentially psychological view of reality. This is not to speak for any specific theory or behavioral treatment, but rather the need to internalize our responsibility, to see the silent origin of choice within, before we can move through the outer world with understanding, effectiveness and perhaps compassion for self and others. That myth has become essentially psychological is not to imply that all things are psychological; rather it is to suggest that our knowledge of all things originates in the psyche.

A psychological view of myth does not degrade myth nor does it promote psychology per se. Myth has always been the bearer of psychic values. With the decline of mythic sensibility, those values have withdrawn into the unconscious of individuals and the tribe, or it has been projected onto outer events and institutions. Thus they must be addressed consciously lest unconscious values take charge. We cannot afford to be driven by unconsciousness, so we are obliged to adopt a psychological view of reality in order to discern the topography of our time. The forces once contained by myth have become the social pathologies of modernism.

To see myth psychologically is not to psychologize, that is, to say that something is *only* psychological. Rather it is to acknowledge that a psychological view is all we have left. It is based on the recognition that the same great patterns are working their way through our lives as once animated the lives of our ancestors. Where those energies were once mediated by vital images, sustained narratives that we call myth, now we are obliged to own them as emanating from ourselves. We are not simple enough, as a civilization, to accept the literalism of myth or suffer the reification of those energies. As we cannot revivify mythologems that once moved generations, so we cannot afford the potential disasters of projecting those energies unconsciously. Through the projection of the shadow onto a *Fuerher*, a whole world may burn.

Since we cannot step back into simplicity, and cannot revive images once the energy that animated them has departed, and since we cannot afford to live unconsciously, we are obliged to attempt a psychological reading of our world. This may feel inadequate; it is certainly less affectively charged than being swept up in the awesomeness of an archetype, but it is our responsibility to become conscious of what is already true, that is, what is already at work within the individual and within history.

A century ago Freud and Jung found that they had to evolve a new language, a new way of relating to the sufferings of their patients. They realized that they were treating those who had fallen between the cracks opened by the erosion of institutional religion and the limitations of medical science. Their task was to discern the wounds to the soul which had incarnated in the venues of body, behavior and affect. To track such energies they had to discern the movement of inner currents.

We in the modern era are similarly obliged to read psychologically, that is, discern the movement of soul, whose invisible traces were once cloaked in the guise of myth. This requires great integrity and brings a measure of dignity and freedom to the one who becomes more conscious. And, no small thing, that person is less dangerous to self and society.

2
The Eternal Return and the Heroic Quest

The great paradigm shift that lies at the very core of modernism is the loss of mythic connection to the cosmos. The incarnation of meaning, once carried by myth and myth-sustaining institutions, has gone within, receded, as Jung said, from Olympus to the solar plexus, from worship to psychopathology.

Within this paradigm shift many other relocations of meaning are transpiring. One of the most awesome is the reevaluation of the role of the individual. (Jung's articulation of individuation, a modern myth, will be addressed later). It is generally assumed today, for example, that individuals are responsible for creating meaning in their lives. Anyone who shuns this terrible freedom will be judged dependent and psychologically immature. An important subparadigm shift is the loosening and redefinition of gender-based roles. This evolving dialogue is liberating men and women from the historic definitions that constricted their energies and wounded their souls.

In this chapter we are going to examine two important mythic patterns: the great round or eternal return—the cycle of sacrifice, the life-death-rebirth dialectic—and the quest or hero's journey, the movement from innocence to experience, from naivete to wisdom, from identification to individuation. In fact, it could be argued that all mythology is an amplification of these two great themes, albeit with infinite variations.

Historically, the myth of the eternal return was associated with the Great Mother Goddess, and the quest was associated with the Sky Father, the solar hero. Both genders participate in the cycle of life-death-rebirth, and both are obliged to undertake the journey toward selfhood. If the imagery in the following pages seems gender-bound, it is not so intended but rather draws from historic imagery that naturally enough arose out of the experience of the personal mother as the source of life and the personal father as the carrier of artificially invented culture. These personal identifications, projected onto the cosmos, led to the two great mythic cycles. Both men and women carry these crucial processes within and both must become more conscious of the tasks they imply.

The erosion of the great myths of Earth Mother and Sky Father has left us to search privately for images to guide and support the soul and link it to the cosmic drama. Without such linkage we are doomed to a life of superficiality. To experience one's life in depth, as part of a larger context, is the central contribution of myth, which, as Jung points out, "explained to the bewildered human being what was going on in his unconscious."[85]

Jung's observation is profound; it reveals why he and Freud and other founders of depth psychology turned to myth and mythic processes, for example in working with dreams. Such images helped render the invisible world visible. Myth is a dynamic structure, it would seem, which animates images that symbolically replicate energies and processes within a person. As Jung explains,

> The archetypes are the numinous, structural elements of the psyche and possess a certain autonomy and specific energy which enables them to attract, out of the conscious mind, those contents which are best suited to themselves. The symbols act as *transformers,* their function being to convert libido from a "lower" to a "higher" form.[86]

Thus myth enables one to feel a sense of spiritual "locus," and presents images that support and direct transformative energies, lending coherence to the random chaos of life. Since these two great mythic themes have become more and more remote from lived experience, we are obliged to make conscious the issues they dramatize in our lives.

Eternal Return: Sacrifice, Death and Rebirth

The myth of the eternal return is a lunar association: shape-changing, protean waxing and waning, disappearances and reappearances. It embodies the cyclic nature of nature, the rhythm and return of human experience.

Nearly thirty years ago I asked a class to write a poem, in order to experience directly that poetry was much more than pretty thoughts, much more than a sing-song rhythm, and that great labor was required to produce what Picasso described as art which conceals art. It was autumn, the

---

[85] *Symbols of Transformation,* CW 5, par. 466.
[86] Ibid., par. 344.

ground strewn with October's dying vegetation, the crack and tang of on-coming November in the air. In a class of about thirty students, fully twenty of them chose to compare the changing season to the cycle of human life. In fact, comparing the human life cycle to movements in nature is not only obvious, because we are part of that nature, but a cliché precisely because the analogy is repeatedly experienced in our bones.

Virtually all poets have turned to this analogy, from Dylan Thomas in "Fern Hill," where he recognizes that he is no longer in the spring of his life, to Gerard Manley Hopkins in "Spring and Fall: To a Young Child," where the poet observes the child's somber response to departing leaves and concludes, "It is the blight man was born for, / It is Margaret you mourn for."[87]

The eternal return is part of the cycle of sacrifice *(sacre + facere,* to make sacred), bringing new life through death, plowing under that life might burst forth anew. This great cycle is observed daily as we sit down to eat, having slain plant or animal whose consumption furthers our own life. Eventually we, too, are returned to the earth in the eternal round. So awesome is this, our participation in the great cycle, that our ancestors offered prayers of supplication and then thanks before and after the hunt, and more recently said grace at the dining table. The killing necessary for life is thus rendered sacred because it is not random or gratuitous; it is part of a larger pattern. The recognition that such pattern will consume us too ought surely to be part of every eating experience.

The myth of the eternal return is associated with the culture of the Goddess of the Great Round. She in turn was associated with procreation and nurturance, with transformation through the many passages of life, but she was also known as the weaver of fate. Traces of the worship of the goddess go back at least as far as 25,000 years and clearly antedate the worship of male deities. The central mythologem of the goddess is the cyclic nature of nature—the seasons, the tides, the systole and diastole of the blood stream. Goddesses flourished throughout the ancient world as manifestations of the archetype of the Great Mother, as local *numina* of land and water.

---

[87] *Norton Anthology of Poetry,* p. 857.

Most of all, the mythologem embodies the mystery of the life force. As Jung suggested of the Great Mother, she is "the mysterious root of all growth and change; the love that means homecoming, shelter, and the long silence from which everything begins and in which everything ends."[88] Implied by that last phrase, however, is the fact that the Great Mother also devours her progeny. She is both birth and grave, lustfulness and cancer—all aspects of one thing bound for one end.

Increasingly the worship of the Great Mother was replaced in the souls of nomadic peoples by images of quest rather than the centered round, by the more mobile sky gods, solar deities. So, by the third millennium, the organizing images of the Great Mother were often supplanted by the Sky Father, patriarchy replacing matriarchy.

We sense an echo of this often violent paradigm shift in the Judeo-Christian myth of the first pair being expelled from Eden as a result of their encounter with the fateful serpent. The serpent, due to its primal contact with the earthy Great Mother and its ability to renew itself annually by shedding its skin, received the projection of the eternal return, and by its intimation of the old consciousness was cast as the villain of the Fall from grace. Indeed, the Fall *is* a fall from grace, for what is lost is not innocence but connectedness. The sense of psychic locus in the bosom of the Great Mother is extirpated. It is the bitter birth into the consciousness of separation and the presentiment of mortality. The movement from matriarchal to patriarchal consciousness is as traumatic, and as necessary, as the separation of the child from its mother. It is the necessary prerequisite for consciousness and for development. But one is then thrust into the world without a home, forever.

The experience of the goddess is threefold—maiden, mother and crone, each representing a stage of consciousness and each a stage of natural development. Echoes of the triple goddess Car, for example, linger just beneath the surface. We hear her footsteps from Carthage to Khartoum to Carpathia, and intuit her incarnations in carnal, carmine, cardinal, cardiac and Karma. We experience her ancient permutations in Innin, Inanna, Nana, Nut, Anat, Anahita, Ishtar, Isis, Ishara, Asherah, Ashtart, Astarte,

---

[88] "Psychological Aspects of the Mother Archetype," *The Archetypes and the Collective Unconscious,* CW 9i, par. 172.

Attoret, Attar and Hathor. We observe a matinal dismemberment of Ceres, goddess of grains, in our morning cereal. We stir with Ishtar's estrogen in monthly cycle even as Easter is observed through the gathered Marys at the foot of the cross who are recalling the son to the Mother.

The central meaning of the experience of the Great Mother is the cycle of sacrifice. The truth the goddess embodies is that the life-death cycle is fed by sacrifice, that all life feeds on other life and then serves to feed another. We can accept this intellectually, but the emotional implications are rather closer to home. (Just hours ago my cat brought a live but mutilated mouse into the house as her trophy. My dog, Shadrach, barks at these intrusions and I fling them outside, not wanting to be reminded of nature naturing.) As the goddess embodies all life, she must sacrifice all her children that life might renew. The sacrifice of the divine child is a recurrent motif in Western myth: Aphrodite sacrifices Attis, Cybele sacrifices Adonis, Isis sacrifices Horus, and Mary stands beneath the tree of life and death at Golgotha, the place of the skull. As Christ hung on that tree, so Wotan before him on Yggdrasil, the spinning axle of the world, as did Attis and Marsyas of antiquity. M. Esther Harding reminds us:

> In these myths the mother is not one, she is dual. She has two aspects: in her light aspect she is compassionate, filled with maternal love and pity, and in her dark aspect she is fierce and terrible and will not tolerate childish dependence.[89]

The Hindu goddess Kali, whose name means "black time" and whose neck is festooned with sculls, embodies this duality as well. So, when the goddess sacrifices her issue, she is saying *hoc est corpus meum,* "Here is my body, eat! Here is my blood, drink!"

There is, perhaps, no image more horrific to the imagination than the sacrifice of one's own children. We may acknowledge that ancient cultures sometimes sacrificed their children as a form of "sympathetic magic," making a tacit deal with the gods: "We offer you our first, our best, in return for your sacrifice of your bounty, your harvest." We note that moment in the evolution of human consciousness when Abraham, torn in heart and soul, offered up his son Isaac in sacrifice to Yahweh. Yahweh

---

[89] *Woman's Mysteries, Ancient and Modern,* p. 193.

stayed his hand, but the fact remains, we must, to receive something, sacrifice something. And we are haunted, in a century of materialism and acquisition, by the imperative of Jesus, "Whosoever seeks to gain his life will lose it; but whosoever loses his life will gain it."[90]

So the drama of the cycle of sacrifice, quid pro quo of the gods, reverberates down through history. From the Old Norse epic Edda comes the cry of Wotan:

> I ween that I hung on the windy tree,
> hung there for nights full nine.
> With the spear I was wounded, and offered
> was to Wotan, myself to myself,
> On the tree that none may ever know
> what root beneath it runs.[91]

We cannot help but see the parallels with the sacred *Totentanz* (death-dance) of Golgotha. The "windy tree" is the cross of the Nazarene carpenter. The "nine nights" is the triplicate three, the number symbolic of transformation and replicated in the three days of the Easter sacrifice. The spear thrust into the side is the wound from the collective which both mother's sons suffer. In Wotan's return to himself we hear the echoes of the first sentence of the Gospel of John: "In the beginning was the Word, and the word was with God, and the Word was God."[92] Yggdrasil was the world tree, the omphallic, central spinning axis of the world. When the Jew at Pesach says, "Next year in Jerusalem," he or she is affirming the mythic axis whose center is in our hearts and souls. The Hebrew prophet Jesus suggested that the kingdom of God is within; his disciple Paul said, "Not Christ, but Christ in me."[93] The Sioux shaman Black Elk observed that Harney Peak, the central mountain, is in South Dakota, and it is everywhere.[94]

The ineluctable demand of the gods calls us back to sacrifice, something for something. Wotan (Odin) is a savior figure who suffers vicariously.

---

[90] Luke 17: 33, New English Bible.
[91] Quoted in Joseph Campbell, *The Mythic Image*, p. 419.
[92] John 1: 1, New English Bible.
[93] Quoted in Joseph Campbell, *This Business of the Gods . . .*, p. 135.
[94] Ibid., p. 30.

On the sacred tree he sacrifices an eye and in return is vouchsafed the runes, the alphabet of Nordic Europe. In Greek myth Prometheus, whose name suggests the knowledge of the future, steals fire, the creative spark, making possible culture and the industry of *homo faber.* In return he is condemned to lie chained to a rock in the Caucasus and have his side gnawed by a vulture, as Jesus and Wotan were similarly wounded. So, in order to gain something, something vital must be sacrificed. Wotan sacrifices his eye, as Oedipus his, so that we might transcend darkness, gain insight.

In 1777 Captain Cook reported that on the island paradise of Tahiti he saw the eye removed from a living celebrant and presented to the chief of the tribe to eat. "Here is my body, eat!"[95] In the Egyptian *Book of the Dead* we read, "Take to thyself the Eye of Horus, which thou tasteth."[96] So it seems the gods have ordained that the selected ones symbolically sacrifice something vital so that the rest of us may feed and be transformed. To see the eye of Wotan, or the eye of Horus, resting above the pyramid on the American dollar bill is to realize how we have cheapened the trade for the insight of the gods.

*

The archetype of the eternal return stirs repeatedly, not only down the long corridors of history but in modern dreams. In my years as a Jungian analyst certain dreams remain unforgettable. A fifty-one-year-old woman was deeply religious in intent but party to no institutional creed. The week of Passover and Easter she dreamt she went to a theologian to ask the meaning of Easter. The theologian defined the concept and the dogma, and then the dreamer replied, "I could only understand the meaning of Easter if I were to bear the baby Jesus, from my own womb, on the cross."

This is a most remarkable dream. The woman was feeling a need that typically arises in the second half of life: the need to redefine oneself, to relocate oneself in the context of a larger journey. If the purpose of the first half of life is to gather sufficient ego energy to leave home and set out into the world, the purpose of the second half is to align that ego with the

---

[95] Campbell, *Mythic Image,* pp. 430f.
[96] Ibid., p. 450.

grander energies of the cosmos. Then the ego dialogues not with society but with the Self and the gods.

In the dream the woman listens to the ratiocination of the theologian, but it does not connect with her soul. It is dogma, not felt experience. And so, spontaneously, she says that understanding comes only from personal experience. She must bear the baby herself, which means it must be born from within. Yet her child when born is already on the cross, a strange anachronism. It would seem that her child would be born in order to be sacrificed. "In my beginning is my end," as T.S. Eliot expressed it.[97]

The archetype of the dying god is a contradiction, an oxymoron. How can a god die? A god dies when the principle it dramatizes has been forgotten or superseded. A god dies when the dynamic principle it embodies has lost its energy. A god dies when that energy departs the vessel of concept or image and goes underground or takes on a new form.

Intuitively the dreamer above had grasped the sacred meaning of Easter, that the god has come to die, to be plowed back under so that new life might emerge, to be eaten "that ye might have life and have it abundantly."[98] The child, representing all humankind, has been born to a high destiny.

The same week I heard this woman's dream I read in the *International Herald Tribune* that some American yahoos had been arrested for destroying an image of an Easter rabbit in a mall, saying "no pagan symbol" would be allowed to contaminate their religious holiday. But we must remember that Easter is connected to Ishtar and estrogen, and that in the rabbit's fecundity, as in the phallos of the May Pole, we recover the archetypal meaning of this holiday of life, birth, sacrifice, death and transfiguration. These religious fanatics were apparently unaware that their savior was rather late in the sacred parade of sons slain vicariously to recycle the child to the Great Mother.

Rather than contaminate Easter, the pagan symbols underscore its archetypal meaning of which Christianity is but one expression. The dreamer intuited the deeper meaning of the holiday—the archetype of the divine child, born to suffer and die, then to be resurrected, to live again in

---

[97] "East Coker," line 1, in *The Complete Poems and Plays of T.S. Eliot*, p. 123.
[98] John 10: 10, New English Bible.

the souls of believers. In the spontaneous, symbolic imagery of her dream she perhaps had more of a religious experience, that is, a depth encounter with the mysteries, than do those who troop to houses of worship or burn papier-mâché rabbits.

From whence come such mysteries, such images? They are as mysterious as our dreams. But they are real, as dreams are real. Do they all come from the gods, from the psyche? Are we the unconscious creators of such images or merely the recipients of hermetic conundrums? I do not know, but I suspect we are the vehicles for truths that may be difficult to understand but with which we are obliged to harmonize if we wish to live meaningfully. Myths tell us what is really going on both within ourselves and within the cosmos. As a seventeenth-century alchemical manuscript expressed it, "All that is above also is below."[99]

The archetype of the eternal return, the great round, dramatizes a revelation of the highest mystery—that under the guise of death there is a secret unity of life. This notion has been woven into many symbolic representations. The rite of the scapegoat and the vicarious sacrifice of the tragic protagonist are illustrations. The tragic hero carries the accumulated pathology of the family or the city-state and his or her *sparagmos,* the rending and eating of the sacrificial lamb in ancient rite, serves to feed the soul and liberate from death. Later, in Christianity, the Christ (which means the anointed or chosen one), serves as the lamb of God, the *Agnus Dei,* who takes on the collective burden of sin and guilt and redeems through his sacrifice. *(Agnus Dei qui tolles peccata mundi.)*

The unfolding of this drama lends depth to life, which is the purpose of ritual. The theologian Paul Tillich once observed that the greatest sin of modernism was not evil, though evil is abundant enough, but rather the barren triviality that preoccupies us.[100] Recall how clearly Jung has spoken to this dilemma, pointing out that individuals are only connected to the meaning of life when they "feel they are living the symbolic life, that they are actors in the divine drama."[101]

---

[99] Often quoted by Jung; see, for instance, "The Psychology of the Transference," *The Practice of Psychotherapy,* CW 16, par. 384.

[100] *Theology of Culture,* p. 24.

[101] See above, p. 11.

In the arid landscape of modernism, whose only monuments, observed T.S. Eliot, are "asphalt highways and a thousand lost golf balls,"[102] the recovery of that depth principle helps heal the world wound and redirect the soul.

*

A number of years ago, while visiting my son in St. Petersburg, Florida, I went to the Salvador Dali Museum. His surrealistic paintings were once shocking but have since entered the mainstream of modern culture. On the wall of the museum is his observation: "The difference between me and a madman is that I am not mad."

Raised in the culture of Spain, Dali was imbued with the dogma of his tribe, namely Roman Catholicism, yet his vision often taps into the broader Mediterranean mythos. As I walked through the museum, I was struck by a thought like Jung might have had when first he walked through the wards of the schizophrenics at the Burgholzli Klinik in Zurich: "I have been here before; I have seen this before." What I saw in several of the paintings was Dali's intuition that beneath the patriarchal character of the Spanish Church courses the deeper drama of the Great Mother.

In one painting of the Last Supper Dali depicts two levels of the ritual *sparagmos,* the breaking of the body and its transformation in the souls of his disciples. Both planes are evident: the earthly Jesus and the divine child born to be torn and transfigured. In a scene of the crucifixion, Dali depicts the ancient drama with Mary at Christ's feet as both Great Mother and earthly peasant. Dali's treatment dramatizes the deeper mythic movement, the great round. In a painting of the discovery of the new world by Columbus the same theme emerges—the child descends from the Sky Father, passes through the Great Mother, enters the world of action, and through suffering is transfigured—returning through the great round.

In a painting titled *The Hallucinogenic Toreador,* one sees the Mother (often portrayed in Dali's paintings by his wife Gala) at upper left, overseeing the ritual of the *sparagmos* once again. For those of us not raised in Spain, bull fights may seem gratuitously violent, but as Hemingway

---

[102] "Choruses from 'The Rock'," in *The Complete Poems and Plays of T.S. Eliot,* p. 103.

demonstrated in *Death in the Afternoon,* the bull fight is an art form grounded in mythic history, the ritual sacrifice of the bull, a recurrent symbol in the Mediterranean culture of the Great Mother. Thus the slaying of the bull is analogous to the Eucharist and the *Agnus Dei.* The bull offers up its body and blood, as does the toreador who enacts a stylized *Totentanz.* Each is a child of the Great Mother, each a part of the inexorable transit of the great round, the recurrent setting forth and the eternal return.

What Dali does in these and many other paintings is to plumb the depths of stock images and restore their archetypal undergirding. It is essential to understand what that archetypal dimension is. Simply put, the purpose of the cycle of blood and sacrifice, death and rebirth, is to enable us to participate in the suffering of the elected one, and through that suffering to be lifted out of the random horrors of life onto a mythologically appropriated plane of mystery and meaning.

There is no meaning to life unless one is in touch with its archetypal roots. In Dali's paintings, such seemingly mundane secular events as a colonial voyage and a bull fight are revealed to have profound depth. The randomness of life, the horror of death and dissolution are mediated. The individual alienated soul is relocated in a grander context. Death is slain and one is called to participate in a sacred drama, the ever-changing but eternal return.

*

In his autobiography Jung writes:

> I have frequently seen people become neurotic when they content themselves with inadequate or wrong answers to the questions of life. They seek position, marriage, reputation, outward success or money, and remain unhappy and neurotic even when they have attained what they were seeking. Such people are usually confined within too narrow a spiritual horizon. Their life has not sufficient content, sufficient meaning. If they are enabled to develop into more spacious personalities, the neurosis generally disappears.[103]

Jung's point is essential for us to consider. In the shamanic tradition of healing, what we call neurosis was perceived as the alienation of the indi-

---

[103] *Memories, Dreams, Reflections,* p. 140.

vidual from his or her mythic roots. (Psychologists were called "alienists" in the last century.) Therefore the shaman would frequently chant the creation stories and the foundation myths of the tribe so as to reconnect the lost soul to its roots, its archetypal rhythms. If we live within too narrow a myth, that is, a set of images provided by our culture or family of origin which constricts the health of the soul, we suffer that self-alienation we call neurosis.

The etymological Indo-Germanic root *angh,* from which we get the words *anxiety, angst, anger* and *angina,* means "constriction"; the constriction of the organism by too narrow a myth deforms and defeats the soul. We must consider our own place in the great round. Jung asserts that neurosis is "the suffering of a soul which has not discovered its meaning."[104] Thus we are obliged to find meaning lest life be sterile and absurd. To affirm our participation in the depth and breadth of the mortal transit, we must affirm not only the aesthetic appeal of the noisy geese honking their way south in the autumn but also our participation in that great round. What is eternal is not the goose; it is the cycle. What is eternal is not the individual witness; it is the cycle. The felt apprehension of our participation in the great round lifts us out of the random horror of carnivorous nature onto that mythic plane of meaning.

The awareness that there is a depth dimension to all that we experience enlarges our vision, relocates us in a timeless zone. Participation in the great round retains both the mystery it represents and the dignity of those who die. An awareness of such an intricate rhythm was more readily available to our ancestors and would today help compensate for the sterility of modernist ideologies. Such mythic representations activate psychic energy and redirect the soul toward healing. We cannot heal ourselves by act of will, intellect or right conduct, but we can experience healing when we are in harmony with some great rhythm. Then we are living the symbolic life and find consonance with the universe, rather than a void.

The exiled Indian prince Gautama undertook his journey and came at last, beneath another sacred tree, to see; in seeing he became a Buddha (Sanskrit *buddh,* to see). What he saw was that all life is suffering and that

---

104 "Psychotherapists or the Clergy," *Psychology and Religion,* CW 11, par. 497.

the cause of suffering is the desire of the ego to control life, most of all to control one's mortality. The secret of living well, according to all the great mythic systems, is to live in accord with the will of the gods, in harmony with the Tao. In so doing, we align ourselves with wisdom greater than our intelligence, and rhythms greater than our transient motions.

We moderns, enjoined to see the purpose of life as acquisition, more deeply suffer the inevitability of loss. If we live long enough, everyone about whom we care will leave us. If we do not live long enough, we will have left them. To transform loss into "letting go," to identify with "the great coming and going," to replace acquisition with the capacity to relinquish, is to participate in the secret wisdom of the Great Mother. Hers is the oldest of truths, a mystery we intimate in the sacred *OM* of mother, myth and mystery.

In his autobiography Jung offers the decisive question to ask of a patient and of ourselves:

> Is he related to something infinite or not? That is the telling question of his life. . . . If we understand and feel that here in this life we already have a link with the infinite, desires and attitudes change. In the final analysis, we count for something only because of the essential we embody, and if we do not embody that, life is wasted.[105]

The capacity to stand in relationship to something deeper than our consciousness, to something longer than our life span, is to feel the worth and weight of the soul. Thus Jung once defined life as "a short episode between two great mysteries, which yet are one."[106]

To render this episode as luminous as possible is to rediscover in the movements of soul, in the visitations in the body, in the spectral presences in our dreams, the trace of the gods. We carry them, and they carry us. The cycle of sacrifice, which terrifies the ego, supports and heals the soul.

The Journey of the Hero

These sentences are being written just hours after the televised accusations, flight and arrest of O.J. Simpson. That a nation could be so focused, so captivated by the plight of a single person, is of no small mo-

---

[105] *Memories, Dreams, Reflections,* p. 325.
[106] *Letters,* vol. 1, p. 483.

ment for the work of the soul. Such energy comes always from soul, that is, from some region deeper than one is aware of. Why such energy, why such projections? Is O.J. a hero, of some or any kind?

The idea of the hero, like the idea of myth, has grown rather tattered and needs to be consciously refurbished. Just as myth has become synonymous in modern culture with the idea of falsehood, so hero has deteriorated to the notion of "large, bold, celebrated." For our purposes, O.J. is not a hero but a celebrity who had at least his fifteen minutes of fame and more, and whose ride down the Los Angeles freeway may indeed enter the realm of legend just as Bonnie and Clyde and Dillinger and Jesse James and other low-lifes have stirred the popular imagination, an imagination excited and fed today by instant feedback, books within a week of the event, and made-for-television movies within months. Celebrities receive the projections of the masses and are carriers of their unconscious drives and unlived lives.

People are shocked by the thought that a man with a wonderfully warm persona, accomplishments on the field and in the media, might also murder his wife. Those familiar with Jung's concept of the shadow may be shocked but not surprised, for they know the murderer lurks within all of us. Readers of the Bible will have seen the dark side of King David. Readers of Jung's "Answer to Job" will have encountered the dark side of God. Readers of Hawthorne and Melville will have observed the work of the Devil in the religious communities of New England and on the tempest-tossed sea. Sycophants of television evangelists are shocked and then titillated by the peccadilloes of their leaders.

Everywhere, from newsstands to television, our unlived lives are projected onto the high and mighty. Often such a figure is embraced and then easily discarded when his or her foibles are revealed. An O.J. seemed to lead the magical life of celebrity and southern California. The allegation that he had beaten and threatened his wife, and ultimately killed her, was shocking because one is not supposed to carry both the projections of a solar hero on the one hand and do the work of darkness on the other. Thus one may say that an O.J. ceases to be an ordinary human being who can awaken any given morning with murder in his heart, but a plastic, one-sided carrier of projections from those who are profoundly out of touch with the universality of the shadow.

Yet, O.J. is very much the hero when we look at him in the way Homer and the Greek tragedians would have. He was a man raised up, carrier of the hopes and values of his tribe, doer of great deeds, but haunted by a tragic flaw that proves his undoing. When we examine Greek tragedies we see that the Chorus, which represents wisdom and the point of view of the author, tells us how much the hero is set up by fate. Fate is an implacable force in the universe, a force which no one, king or commoner, can escape. Fate rewards some with special gifts, the tendons and tissue to run 40 yards in 4.3 seconds, for example, or the ability to see a whole football field at a glance and cut back against the grain. But just as energy flows toward the talent, or the adaptation to life, so other parts of the psyche are neglected and fall into the unconscious. Those split-off parts lie there, wait for the right circumstances, and then reassert their autonomy over consciousness. They repossess consciousness, often in exaggerated ways because they have been repressed. "Frustrated Postal Employee Shoots Nine; Co-workers Say He Was a Nice Guy, Quiet, Kept to Himself."

Accordingly, as a person disconnects from unwanted aspects of the psyche, so he or she will be at the mercy of their revenge. One will unconsciously make choices out of this framework, and then have to bear the consequences. Thus the Greek tragedians depicted in their trilogies the history of a house, that is, a family, through three generations. The wounds of the first generation hurt the second, who in turn wound the next, until someone suffers enough to come to consciousness and break the chain. Fate provides the initial wounding and the flawed parenting of each subsequent generation, and yet all are responsible for the lives they have chosen—as we too are responsible for our choices and their consequences. That one has made choices from a wounded vision, a flawed perspective, is usually clear only in retrospect, with the consciousness our suffering has brought.

The wounded vision was called *hamartia* by the Greeks, and accounts for how the best and brightest are their own worst enemies no less than those who have been given few advantages by fate. The Oedipus of Sophocles is a supreme example of a man whom Fate afflicted and yet, given what was unconscious in his character, made choices that doomed him. He expresses this paradox of "fated freedom" when he proclaims:

> It was Apollo, friends, Apollo,
> that brought this bitter bitterness, my sorrows to completion.
> But the hand that struck me
> was none but my own.[107]

That Oedipus is the paradigm of the gifted person choosing from his flawed and partial prism of consciousness is made clear by the Chorus:

> What man, what man on earth wins more
> of happiness than a seeming
> and after that turning away?
> Oedipus, you are my pattern of this,
> Oedipus, you and your fate![108]

Another recent example of the tragic hero was played out on the world stage by former President Nixon. Wounded by the losses of his youth, he lent himself to the power complex and achieved the most powerful office in the world. Yet, that *hamartia,* that wounded vision remained insecure and unable to shake the haunting of history, so he made decisions, chose henchmen and set in motion events that would lead to his disgrace. As he stood in the Oval Office of the White House to resign, he dwelt on his deprived childhood and the mother who had stood by him. O.J., alleged abuser and murderer, drove back to his home in order to see his mother. The fated power of such relationships drove these men to heights and wounded them in such fashion as to lead to their undoing.[109]

The story of the tragic hero touches us because he or she exemplifies the dilemma of each of us. Fate wounds and surrounds, and from that intersection between fate and character history is generated. This history is both personal and collective, for often such a figure embodies the hopes and aspirations, as well as the shadow, of a whole people. As an oft-repeated maxim of my youth had it, "In Adam's Fall, sinned we all." Adam, as the

---

[107] Sophocles, *Oedipus the King,* p. 68.

[108] Ibid., p. 64.

[109] See my book *Under Saturn's Shadow: The Wounding and Healing of Men,* chap. two, "Dragon Dread," for the way in which the fated power of the mother-son nexus leads to men's fear of the feminine within them and the woman outside. This complex is a universal example of how the interplay between fate, unconsciousness and choice leads to suffering.

primal man, served as the paradigm for the human condition. Through his hubris he illustrated the all-too-human propensity to inflate consciousness by telling it what it wanted to hear. In *The Poetics* Aristotle suggested that we are drawn to witness such tragic drama, be it on stage or on the field of history, because we need the catharsis of very powerful emotions, namely pity and fear. Our pity is evoked, and released, as we identify with the tragic suffering of the protagonist and fear that we are at risk as well.

Having seen the humbling of their best and brightest, the Greek Chorus summarizes the tragic dilemma of all heroes, all humans: "Count no mortal happy till / he has passed the final limit of his life secure from pain."[110] Or think on Shakespeare's mythic king, Richard II. Having sought all and lost all he reminds us that

> within the hollow crown
> That rounds the mortal temples of a king
> Keeps Death his court and there the antic sits,
> Scoffing his state and grinning at his pomp,
> allowing him a breath, a little scene,
> to monarchize. . . .
> Infusing him with self and vain conceit . . .
> subjected thus,
> How can you say to me, I am a king?[111]

Such figures, larger than life, like O.J. and Richard Nixon, ultimately play out the psychic dilemma of all humans. When consciousness neglects the shadowy parts and inflates its own importance, the gods grow interested, draw near, and bring about the restoration of balance.

No hero, perhaps, more usefully serves us than the one who reminds us of our limitations, of the gap between the human and the gods. It might be useful, then, to define the hero as *one who expands our sense of the possible and yet reminds us of the necessary boundaries of the human condition.*

The most easily observed example would of course be that person who is able to transcend physical boundaries, the explorer or astronaut for instance. But equally, explorations of the spirit, of intellect and of creativity

---

110 Sophocles, *Oedipus the King,* p. 76.
111 Act 3, scene 2, lines 160-178.

manifest the heroic enterprise. Charles Lindbergh, "The Lone Eagle," captured the world's attention because it was the human capacity to dream and to venture that was being tested in his small cockpit. Over forty aviators had already flown the Atlantic, but Lindbergh was the first to do it alone. It was this dramatization of the solitary venture of the spirit, this courage, endurance, imaginative boldness that knit the continents together. Similarly, Beethoven not only articulated a number of musical ideas, but, like all creators, he expanded the nature of music itself. In each case, the heroic spirit pushed outward the boundaries of the possible. Each heroic effort, then, is an exercise in reimagining the possible, reconfiguring the limits.

Understanding the hero as one who expands our sense of the possible must also require us to distinguish between positive and negative heroes. The butchers of history who led nations into darkness remind us of our shadow. Sometimes the psychotic extends our range of the imaginal resources of mind. A woman today hearing voices telling her to march on the forces of the Establishment would likely be treated for a psychiatric disorder. Joan of Arc, Maid of Orleans, pushed these limits and was made a saint. George Fox wandered mad through the village of Lichfield and created the Society of Friends.

Even a Hitler served to remind us of how the forces of the unconscious could be projected onto a charismatic figure and lead ordinary citizens into a collective madness. We must ponder such examples and recognize how fragile is the individual's sense of ethics and personal responsibility. As the modern has felt the erosion of the hierarchy of sustaining mythic values over the last few centuries, anti-heroes have become ubiquitous, their literary track running from Dostoyevsky and Melville through Eliot's J. Alfred Prufrock, the works of Saul Bellow, Philip Roth and others, to Beckett's two tramps on the roadside.

Many historical figures who suffered calumny and martyrdom were perpetrators of a "holy crime," an offense against collective values that yet offers a timely critique of those values and wins acceptance by the citizens of a later age. Socrates, for example, was condemned to death by his peers for impiety. At the time of his compliance with the sentence, Socrates noted that the just person cannot be rendered unjust by the verdict of others. Justice can neither be given nor removed—it can only be a state of the soul. Thus, such holy criminals as Socrates, Jesus, Martin Luther King, Jr., and others who transgress the norms of local time and place, are heroic because they operate from an enlarged moral vision which subsequently expands the vision of their tribe.

Often ordinary people are summoned at some decisive moment to perform an act wherein they stand in relationship to the enlarged possibilities of the human. On that frontier they might be quite alone, quite misunderstood, quite unrewarded, but they do what they have to do if they are going to be wholly true to themselves. At that moment, as the individual stands before the limitations of fear, he or she represents something universal and through the heroic impulse may carry the human spirit to new heights.

We need now to consider two questions: what constitutes the typical heroic journey, and what is its psychological meaning?

The heroic journey

No single legend will contain all of the motifs of the journey as described herein, but all will illustrate at least one aspect. For example, the hero is always "called," although he or she may not initially understand this as a call or even wish to be called. Odysseus, for example, feigned madness in order to avoid going on the expedition against Troy. He sowed his field with salt, but when his children were placed in front of his plow and he had to exercise rational choice to save them, he was then dragged to his destiny.

The call or summons represents a need for some older value, personal or tribal, to be overthrown. Seldom is the way clear. Certainly it is never easy. The hero must persist, with the greatest obstacle being his or own lethargy, fear and longing for home.

Sometimes the hero will receive critical aid from another—an old crone, a gnome in the forest, a helpful animal, advice remembered from a wise elder, or strengths to draw upon from the tribal memory. The path is strewn with various temptations—the devil of doubt, hope for an easier way, seductions of wealth, power, hedonism. Odysseus, on the long voyage back to Ithaca, had to wrench his men away from the Isle of the Lotus Eaters, whose sweet poppies would ease their pain, and the enchantments of Circe, who would turn them into sensual swine. All of these temptations caused his crew to forget the journey.

Often the hero of such stories sets out on an adventure in the world; sometimes the journey is internal as the hero descends into the depths of the unconscious. If the hero survives the descent—and typically many predecessors did not—and the battle with whatever monsters await in the depths, then he or she is able to undertake the ascent and be transformed. This transformation constitutes a death and rebirth experience. Who the person was, and what his or her conscious world was like, is no more. All is transformed.

Often these struggles have wounded the person. Think of the wounds of Christ and Wotan and Odysseus, for example, wounds through which they were later recognized as heroes. Wounds quicken consciousness and, as we recall from the mythology of the eternal return, are the necessary quid pro quo for enlargement. Frequently there are tokens of this new state—a pot of gold, the hand of the beloved, a new homeland—but these are only the outward vestiges of a changed relationship of soul to cosmos.

The hero attains a new consciousness of the possible and a new relationship to the tribe and to the gods. As tokens of this change are irrelevant to the worth of the transformation of consciousness, such trophies need to be seen metaphorically. Any quest for the trophies themselves would be materialism, seeking the icon instead of the god, and losing the point of it all. While the journey of the hero may take the form of outer adventures, the goal is inner transformation. While the heroic adventures of our tribal memory take some outer form, the same motifs of summons, descent, struggle, wounding and return are part of the everyday life of the individual. To discern that each of us is part of such a rich pattern on a daily basis is to recover the depth principle.

The psychological meaning of the journey

Tom Stoppard wrote an interesting play a number of years ago titled *Rosencrantz and Guildenstern Are Dead.* Rosencrantz and Guildenstern are familiar as very minor characters in *Hamlet.* In Shakespeare's version, Hamlet is of course the tragic hero who is summoned and encounters overwhelming inner resistance to his duty to avenge his father. Finally, at the end of the longest play Shakespeare ever wrote, Hamlet overcomes his lethargy and acts. In the meantime, the transient passages of Rosencrantz and Guildenstern are concluded with the simple remark that they are dead—unimportant if the play is called *Hamlet*, but very important if one is in a play called *Rosencrantz* or *Guildenstern*.

Stoppard follows the thought that each of us is cast into a great drama, a drama in which we may be following an uncertain script but in which, surely, we are summoned to be the protagonist. The denouement of the play is certain—we die. But the meaning of Stoppard's play derives from how and in what fashion the protagonist can come to consciousness and make heroic choices. Certainly Stoppard's twin figures are in the anti-hero mold as they wander about in the uncertain play of their lives, not clear about who they are or what is going on, interrupted once in awhile by some guy named Hamlet who crosses their stage with a sense of his own importance.

Rosencrantz and Guildenstern are prototypes for modern individuals, who, feeling no heroic stature, no sustaining mythos, wander from idea to idea, impulse to impulse, morosely changing channels in the hope of finding something better to watch.

In each of us there is a Hamlet, adrift in the cross-currents of ambivalence, and in each of us a Rosencrantz or Guildenstern. In each of us is the archetype of the hero, the capacity to rise to the challenge of life. If we have an outer hero it is only to remind us of our own imperative. In the acts of another—the one who scales the impossible slope, the one who discovers the new vaccine, the one who articulates a transformative idea, the one who brings beauty into the world—we are reminded of our own calling, our heroic vocation.

Surely the only measure by which we can judge ourselves in the end, or be judged by others, is the degree to which we have heard and responded to the imperative to become ourselves in the face of what would hold us back. The stories of heroes may inspire and guide us, but it is up to each to answer our own call, to individuate. As the old Zen parable has it, "I am looking for the face I had before the world was made." Throughout the land there are those who quietly, daily, answer this call, taking care of their children, going to their burdensome but necessary jobs, fighting self-doubt and fear. Such persons, in their unsung ways, are worthier of admiration than celebrities; heroic others are not meant to divert us from our own journey but rather to remind us of it.

The recurrent leitmotif of the hero's quest implies a voyage from unconsciousness toward consciousness, from tenebrous depths to luminous heights, from dependency to self-sufficiency. That force, that patterning energy (which is what an archetype is), seeks to overthrow the domination of chaos, the sweet seductions of unconsciousness, to achieve ever greater differentiation.

Each morning two grinning gremlins sit at the foot of the bed. One is named Lethargy and one is called Fear. Either will gladly eat us alive.It scarcely matters what one did yesterday in combat with them, for they daily renew their interest in possessing the soul. The energy available to take them on is part and parcel of the hero archetype. In this fashion one can see, then, how universal the hero drama is, for each of us has come to recognize the subtle seduction of comfort and the fears that paralyze like Medusa's gaze. Our life's journey is a series of defeats by these demons, a daily-renewed summons to take them on and play the protagonist in the drama that is our life.

Joseph Campbell's classic, *The Hero With a Thousand Faces*, documents the ubiquity of what he considered the mono-myth of the hero. This central myth seems to have three stages: departure, initiation and return. The departure stage arises when the person is expelled from the community or has outgrown the old dispensation. Then he or she is obliged to wander in strange lands. Descents, ascents and wounding initiate the neophyte into the mysteries of nature and of relationship. The return is seldom back to the old land and never back to the old psychology. Such a return would obviate the journey and annihilate consciousness. Rather the return involves circling back at a higher level. Thus the in-forming image of the quest motif is not a linear movement once and for all time, but rather an evolutionary movement akin to a spiral. This voyage necessarily differentiates a person, develops a new being who may no longer be recognizable by the old tribe or the old values. The hero must bear the burden of loneliness and guilt and, as Jung notes, must give something back:

> Individuation cuts one off from personal conformity and hence from collectivity. That is the guilt which the individuant leaves behind him for the world, that is the guilt which he must endeavour to redeem. He must offer

a ransom in place of himself, that is, he must bring forth values which are an equivalent substitute for his absence in the collective personal sphere.[112]

In this way we see that the heroic imperative summons us all, for not only is the individual created thereby, but such a person becomes a treasure to the tribe. Many have thought that individuation is a form of narcissistic preoccupation. Rather the enlarged person, the one who undertakes and returns from the quest, serves the tribe through challenge, redemption and reinvigoration.

The archetype of the journey is the formalization of the life force, that is, the activation and channeling of libido toward greater development. The greatest risk a person will ever encounter is the subtle seduction of the unconscious, the longing to abide in the known and comfortable. Jung describes such a person:

> Always he imagines his worst enemy in front of him, yet he carries the enemy within himself—a deadly longing for the abyss, a longing to drown in his own source. . . . This regressive tendency has been consistently opposed from the most primitive times by the great psychotherapeutic systems which we know as the religions. They seek to create an autonomous consciousness by weaning mankind away from the sleep of childhood.[113]

If it is true that the great myths and myth-making institutions sought to activate and channel the libido of the individual, then the erosion of such powerful guiding images acts as a psychological abandonment. So we are obliged to be even more conscious of our developmental task, since we must often undertake it in solitude and silence.

The "deadly longing for the abyss" that Jung speaks of is the grinning gremlin Lethargy. The other one, Fear, is natural to the fragile human who works so hard to achieve a measure of security only to find that it is a trap, a stultification of the life force. To grow, to individuate, obliges us to reject that security and move into the unknown. Jung puts it dramatically:

> The spirit of evil is fear, negation. . . . he is the spirit of regression, who threatens us with bondage to the mother and with dissolution and extinc-

---

112 "Adaptation, Individuation, Collectivity," *The Symbolic Life,* CW 18, par. 1095.

113 *Symbols of Transformation,* CW 5, par. 553.

tion in the unconscious. . . . For the hero, fear is a challenge and a task, because only boldness can deliver from fear. And if the risk is not taken, the meaning of life is somehow violated, and the whole future is condemned to hopeless staleness, to a drab grey lit only by will-o'-the-wisps.[114]

*

These, then, are the two great ideas contemporary Westerners must keep in mind—the eternal return and the hero's journey. They must be made all the more conscious in our lives because we are not positioned in a sustaining mythological tradition that activates such imperatives, channels libido and mediates the woe and wonder of it all. Those whose traditions presented them with images of the Great Mother were sustained by "great winds across the sky." We are not.

Perhaps nowhere are we more neurotic, that is, split internally, than over the question of mortality. The culture we have evolved is focused on acquisition, fueled by the power complex and sustained by denial. Mortality is the ultimate in personal loss, before which we are powerless, and that will not in the end be denied. Thus mortality serves as the grand affront to modern Western culture and so we call current medical interventions "heroic measures," as if death were the enemy.

The Tibetan tradition has long seen the transitions between life, death, the period after life, and the period of rebirth as a *bardo,* that is, a time of revelation, of transformation of consciousness. In this tradition the daily meditation on one's mortality is understood not as morbidity but as soul work. The more soul work, the greater the achievement of transformative consciousness. How alien this mindfulness of mortality seems in the midst of the wealth and neurotic preoccupations of modernism. Yet to see one's own life as a chip in the mosaic, a spark in the great fire, a drop in the cosmic sea, is not to deny the individual but to relocate oneself in a divine setting.

For an age of wanderers, such relocation is the final homecoming. Secretary of War Edwin Stanton must have felt this at the moment of Lincoln's passing when he said, "Now he belongs to the ages."[115] The memory

---

[114] Ibid., par. 551.
[115] Noah Andre Trudeau, *Out of the Storm,* p. 226.

of the Great Mother, her cycle of sacrifice, the great round, eternal return, serves as both fate and destiny for all humans. Those who can assimilate this image in their bones will transcend much of the alienation that characterizes our culture.

The other great idea, the hero's journey, reminds us of the countertruth, that a person best serves the great mystery of nature by becoming an individual. The paradox is that the person must be subsumed into the great round and yet is incarnated here in order to differentiate and to develop. In this process the tribe is served, the individual is served, and, in ways we can only surmise, the divine is served as well.

It is folly to identify either of these great truths with gender roles, for both women and men are part of the same universal cycle and have the same imperative to individuate. Both have of course been constrained by the ideologies of gender roles, and hurt in body and soul as a result.

It may be unsettling to feel the wind of existential freedom, solitude and terror, but in that climate choices are made. The modern condition is that of deracination, wandering from ideology to ideology, from fad and fashion to ennui and depression, but the meaning of these two eternal mythological patterns is there to be embraced on an individual basis.

We are each obliged to suffer, to meditate upon, to incarnate, our unique experience of the cycle of sacrifice-death-rebirth, and, equally, to overthrow the gremlins of lethargy and fear to become that which nature so mysteriously offered. When we have taken on this unique yet absolute requirement that we become the protagonist in our own life drama, then we are living heroically. Though we may admire another, we need no hero to live for our vicarious satisfaction. Two characters in Bertolt Brecht's *Galileo* express it:

> Unhappy the land that has no heroes.
> No, unhappy the land that needs heroes.[116]

The poet Rilke eloquently summarized both our peril and our promise in his fourth "Sonnet to Orpheus":

> You have been chosen, you are sound and whole. . . .
> Do not be afraid to suffer, give

---

[116] *Galileo,* scene 13.

the heaviness back to the weight of the earth;
mountains are heavy, seas are heavy.
Even those trees you planted as children
became too heavy long ago—you couldn't carry them now.
But you can carry the winds . . . and the open spaces.[117]

---

[117] Trans. Robert Bly, in Robert Bly, James Hillman and Michael Meade, eds., *The Rag and Bone Shop of the Heart*, p. 100.

3

Eating the Sun

The Spontaneous Generation of Myth

Jung noted that psychology was the last of the modern social sciences to emerge because the task and the insights of psychology were once carried by the great myths.

The founders of modern depth psychology, including Freud and Jung, were psychodynamic in their assumptions and methods. Yet recent studies indicate that only ten per cent of therapists in the United States identify themselves as primarily psychodynamically oriented. Given the modern urge to quantify nearly everything, the majority of therapists have moved toward behavioral modification, cognitive restructuring or pharmacological intervention. While all of these methodologies have their merits, they attract many because they can produce quantifiable results and focus on short-term problem solving, crisis-management and adaptation. They are not about the task of transformation, which is long term, labor intensive, nonquantifiable and perilous to boot.

Many critics debunk the scientific grounding of psychodynamic therapies and some have called them pseudo-religions. Neither of these charges should be denied although they need to be reframed. The psyche functions in symbolic language, and even scientific concepts risk the old heresy of literalization. They need to be understood as symbols, that is, images that point beyond themselves toward movements in the soul. Such terms are metaphors, bridges to the unknown, and only those who have never experienced the dialogue with their own unconscious would claim otherwise.

Psychodynamic therapies arose because of the erosion of the great myths and myth-sustaining institutions. While there are sundry pathologies and symptomatic manifestations, as catalogued in the DSM-IV bible, that do not respond to depth work, the primary wound of modern individuals is often the wound to the soul. Having fallen off the roof of the medieval cathedral, we fell into an abyss. Depth psychology is a process whereby the fractured psyche may heal, whereby one may achieve a personal myth to supplant the bankrupt cultural ideologies. It is not a dogma, but rather a methodology that seeks to facilitate one's encounter with inner transforming powers. It is not New Age but Old Age, as old as the archetypes.

The depth approach to the psyche obliges a serious witness to register awe and trepidation for the dynamic power of the unconscious. The Greeks expressed their respect by dramatizing how a Medea could be so possessed by a god that she would slay her children, how an intelligent man like Oedipus could not know the simplest of things, his own identity, or how a Clytemnestra could be aggrieved mother, scheming politician, adulteress and avenger all at once as she cast a net over her husband Agamemnon and butchered him.

The depth psychologist is obliged hour by hour to wonder at the workings of the psyche—how a dream can weave disparate fragments into a telling critique of conscious life, how the unlived life of a parent works invisibly through the child, how the ego is so easily seduced into hearing what it wishes to hear. And, equally, the analyst wonders at the power of the psyche to heal itself and the inherent movement toward wholeness that survive the most horrific traumas. This awe before the mystery is the daily experience of the analyst or any serious attendant upon the soul.

We are told that out of the average life span we spend six years dreaming. This prodigious endeavor is part of the psyche's teleological intent. Dreams are the inscape of the soul and constitute the myth-making process of the individual. The rich weaving of detail, the bending of the laws of time and place, the synthetic power of new combinations, the rich allusions to previous experience—all are familiar to the student of dreams. Freshly surprising, often puzzling, always mysterious, dream work forever connects us with the mystery. If one is able to track dreams over a period of time, they do indicate movement, do show how a person is working with and through issues. The sum of such dreams constitutes an heroic epic at least as formidable as Homer's or Dante's. The descent into the underworld is there, the fearful monsters, huge cast of characters, the titanic struggles—all the stuff of myth.

Other descents into the underworld produce similar mythic material.

Freud worked mostly with hysterics ("somatoform disorders" in contemporary parlance) and Jung worked first with schizophrenics. Both found that those whom medicine had warehoused were individuals with stories to tell; they merited respect and an effort to understand. The third volume of Jung's Collected Works, *The Psychogenesis of Mental Disease,* is a record of his effort to interpret the meaning that might still be found in the disordered mind. Jung discerned in the first decade of this century what Silvano Arietti described decades later:

> When the pain is so intense that it no longer has access to the level of consciousness, when the thoughts are so dispersed that they are no longer understood by fellow men, when the most vital contacts with the world are cut off, even then the spirit of man does not succumb, and the urge to create may persist. The search, the appeal, the anguish, the revolt, the wish, may all be there and can be recognized in the fog of the emotional storm of the schizophrenic patient and within the crumbling of his cognitive structures.[118]

Even the word *schizophrenia,* like *myth, tragic* and *hero,* has been trivialized, as when a person says, "I feel schizophrenic," when they mean ambivalent. Collectively, the loss of a center for a civilization occasions anarchy, the overthrow of the central order by rebellious factions. (Recall Yeats: "Things fall apart, the center cannot hold / mere anarchy is loosed upon the world.")[119] Individually, the loss of the center—namely the ego, with its ability to process information—together with the loss of affective energy, when experienced in its most extreme form constitutes the disease entity called schizophrenia. (In the first decade of this century, Jung's director, Dr. Eugen Bleuler, coined the word to replace the term *dementia praecox,* "early madness," so-called because of the typical early onset of the disease as opposed to *dementia senilis).*

The etiology of schizophrenia is still a mystery, though there is general agreement that it has a biochemical component. While there are medications that reduce the severity of symptoms, there is no known cure. Severe episodes may be cyclic or occur only once in a life-time, or the condition may be chronic. In any case, the individual suffers a disorientation not un-

---

[118] Arietti, *Interpretation of Schizophrenia,* p. 14.
[119] See above, note 17.

like the experience of moderns who have lost their connection to myth. The shattered lens then renders a vision of world and self so bizarre and ideocentric as to occasion extreme isolation or public repudiation. The notion that the products of such a disordered mind might be meaningful, might serve some teleological function, originated with Jung and was followed up by other bold spirits such as R. D. Laing and John Weir Perry.

Perhaps the most useful delineation of schizophrenia, for our purpose, is to describe it as a family of disorders characterized by profound disturbances of thinking, feeling, perception and identity. Disturbances of thinking are evidenced in inappropriate deductions from experience and/or delusional systems. Feeling disturbances result in profound ambivalence, excessive moodiness, depressive withdrawal and a general sense of alienation. Disturbances of perception manifest in visions or hallucinations. Disturbances of identity, perhaps the most severe of all, point to the center that cannot hold, an ego that can no longer interpret and integrate the contents of outer and inner experience.

A good analogy to the schizophrenic experience is to be found in the comparison to dream life. We all dream, and then awaken to go off to work or wherever. We may remark on the fact that we had a dream or we may disregard it. Life goes on more as less as usual. But the schizophrenic wakes up to a world in which the dream is still dreaming itself; the ego is not strong enough to differentiate between inner and outer reality.

The psyche is often at work toward ends that are mysterious to ego consciousness but meaningful to the soul. Sometimes we experience this in a dream, sometimes through the affect of an activated complex that takes possession of the ego. But in all cases, including the experience of schizophrenia, psyche is at work. As H.G. Baynes asserts,

> It is simply a fact (which can be verified by anyone who studies schizophrenic drawings) that these patients tend to produce certain key drawings in which diagrammatic symbols play a prominent role and that these are subsequently used with effect in the development of the symbolical drama.[120]

Products of the soul in tempest may not be art in the traditional sense,

---

[120] *The Mythology of the Soul*, p. 92.

but what is common to the artist and the schizophrenic is that each comes into proximity with the depths of the psyche, depths essentially inaccessible to reason or discursive language and visible only in symbolic images that point beyond themselves toward the mystery.

The artist, whose mythic prototype was Orpheus, has the need and the courage to descend into the lower world, commune with the forces there, and return to the upper world with song, story or image as a fragile memento of the perilous journey. The schizophrenic, however, remains in those depths, charmed or seized by the dynamic contents of the deep, and the intimations which reach us arrive not as song but as symptom, not as integrated work of art but as fractured meaning. (Think of Dali's observation that the difference between him and a madman was that he was not mad.)

To attend the hallucinogenic voyage of the schizophrenic is to draw close to the mysterious workings of psyche and to observe the symbol-forming powers directly. In such encounters we come closer to the heart of psychic life than intellect or concept can take us. With their respect for dreams and visions, the ancients knew this. What we observe in myth, dream and the imaginal products of schizophrenia draws us closer to the fundamental processes of our inner universe.

Before examining drawings that derive from the schizophrenic experience, let us review the character of what we might call mythwork. For the artist, mythwork expresses an emotional truth symbolically; for the schizophrenic the image *is* the emotional truth, that is, it has a literalism that is not true for the artist. The artist manipulates images, colors, shapes, words or sounds; the schizophrenic is manipulated by the materials with which he or she works. The artist can differentiate different levels of symbolic truth. Dante, for example, consciously employed his metaphor of the descent-ascent archetype at four different levels of meaning. The schizophrenic lives all levels simultaneously. For instance, a man may consider himself the emperor of Rome and account for his reduced circumstances as a momentary lapse of fortune or the misunderstanding of underlings. That his regency is a compensation for those reduced circumstances is not understood but lived out unconsciously, since he is possessed by those contents. A Dante or a Dali may unconsciously employ an archetypal motif or consciously draw upon one, but the experience of the schizophrenic is immediate and idiosyncratic.

The discoveries Freud set out in his *Interpretation of Dreams* are useful in considering the character of mythwork. In dreams the unconscious condenses apparently random events into a concise and inwardly meaningful epiphany. The unconscious subverts the orientation of ego toward person, place and time; it speaks in affectively charged images rather than cognitive contents. Such images incarnate meaning in metaphor and symbol.

To Freud's descriptions of dreamwork Jung added the idea of the collective unconscious, wherein images partake not only of the life of the individual but of the universal as well. He also saw that dreams were not necessarily disguised wish-fulfillment but often a spontaneous commentary by the Self on the dreamer's life. According to Jung, dreams could not only be teleological, promoting the ends of consciousness and wholeness, they were also seeking to compensate for the one-sidedness of conscious adaptations. Thus dreams were purposive and corrective, providing, of course, that one could consciously assimilate their message.

To the degree that the psyche is timeless and embraces all things human, so we must acknowledge that the lives we construct are partial, time-bound, fragmentary. If we lean right in conscious choice, the psyche pushes left in order to center us. Dreams, then, confront us with our unlived lives, not what we are but what we might become, not what we have done but what we have failed to do. As we discern the character and motive of dreamwork, so we may see the same process at work in mythwork. It has been observed that a dream is the mythology of the individual and the myth is the dream of the tribe. Both originate spontaneously from the depths and attest to the self-regulating activities of the psyche. Just as dreams are part of the teleological corrective exerted by the individual psyche, continuing the mysterious mission of nature through each person, so too myth, rising from those same depths, carries the corrective teleology of soul. Accepting the premise that dreams are meaningful, we may intimate that the work of the schizophrenic is meaningful as well, not only in the context of that person's life but also in the life of the tribe, since the individual is the carrier of the universal.

In the next few pages we will be examining drawings by two patients diagnosed as schizophrenic. Both were under twenty years old at the time and had been in school until their thinking process became disorganized and ineffective.

The Iron Butterfly

The first two drawings are by a young woman, age seventeen. Susan, as I shall call her, was the child of a middle-class family with no previous history of mental disorder. She had a normal upbringing with only the usual adolescent storms. While she had experimented with marijuana, she had no history of drug abuse. She started hearing voices while in school, voices that told her she had special gifts of insight and that the world would profit from them. Then one day she took off, walking down the middle of a four-lane highway to visit then President Carter to share her plans for world concord. She was picked up by the police and brought to the local psychiatric hospital, evaluated, medicated and admitted on a twenty-one day involuntary confinement.

Understandably, Susan experienced hospital life as a form of imprisonment. While recognizing that something had gone terribly wrong, she wished above all for her release back to her parents. In addition to receiving drugs and group therapy, she was visited three times weekly by her psychotherapist. She was relatively coherent in her conversation, although her delusions of grandiosity persisted, and she happily agreed to express her feeling state in drawings. Using colored pens she drew a series of figures she identified as "The Iron Butterfly." The drawing shown on the next page is typical.

Susan was drawn to the image of the iron butterfly because it resonated with her experience of her condition. She did not know consciously that one of the etymological roots of psyche is in fact "butterfly," quite possibly because the butterfly, like the soul, is obliged to go through transformative stages before it can attain that fragile, elusive beauty for which it is destined. Yet this fragile, fluttering creature is trapped in the archaic, ferric world. Susan's images are archetypal and she has no conscious awareness of their deeper meaning. The writing on her butterfly expresses the split she feels—hopes for peace" and love" in one area, emptiness and loneliness in another.

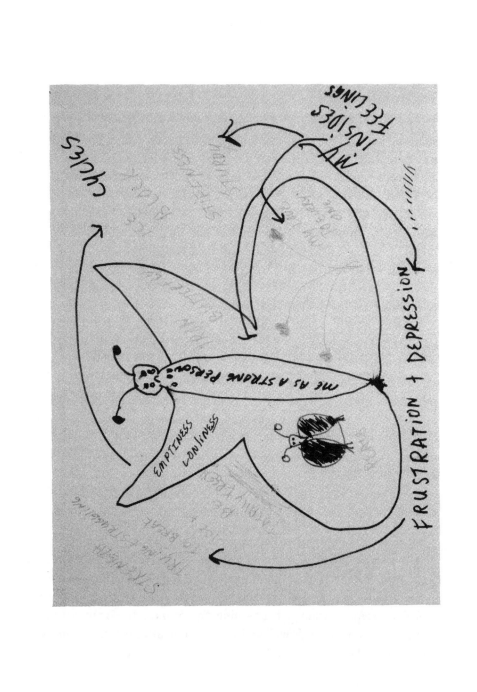

Scratch any teen-ager and such sentiments will emerge, yet the overall context in Susan's case, as we see in the upper right, is encasement in an "ice block," the freezing of psychic movement. At her core we see hope for a favorable development—"me as a strong person"—even though the butterfly has a sorrowful face and weeps. She is able to express her tensions rather well and the splits she feels are identifiable. This is a good sign, as those parts of the psyche that can be identified and dialogued with can ultimately be integrated. Moreover, the theme of fourness recurs in her drawings, a number which archetypally suggests wholeness, that is, the integration of opposites.[121]

Susan's drawing, which she called a self-portrait, was full of mythic import. While she could consciously name the tensions she felt, which augured well for her potential healing, she also experienced a deep torpor and the pull of the archaic. It was perhaps this sense of the power of the unconscious undertow that occasioned her compensatory flights of grandiosity. That her soul was struggling to integrate the separate parts of her life experience, that it was seeking to transcend the bonds of the archaic world, is of course the universal hero's journey. However, the confluence of affective and biochemical forces had drained her life energy and enervated the ego.

In a Dark Wood

Recall the first lines of Dante's descent into the underworld: "Midway in life's journey, I found myself in a dark wood, having lost the way."[122] Though Susan was still in her teens, it is this archetypal motif that she illustrated in another series of drawings, of which the one on the next page is representative.

Readers of literature or mythology, and students of dreams, will quickly recognize motifs in this drawing. Susan places herself, "M-me," at the center of a quadrated structure. So often forest and ocean, in their primal, trackless ways, serve as archetypal symbols for the unconscious. In

---

[121] The alchemical Axiom of Maria comes to mind, often mentioned by Jung as a paradigm of the individuation process: "One becomes two, two becomes three, and out of the third comes the one as the fourth." (See, for instance, *Psychology and Alchemy,* CW 12, par. 26)

[122] *The Comedy of Dante Alighieri,* p. 8.

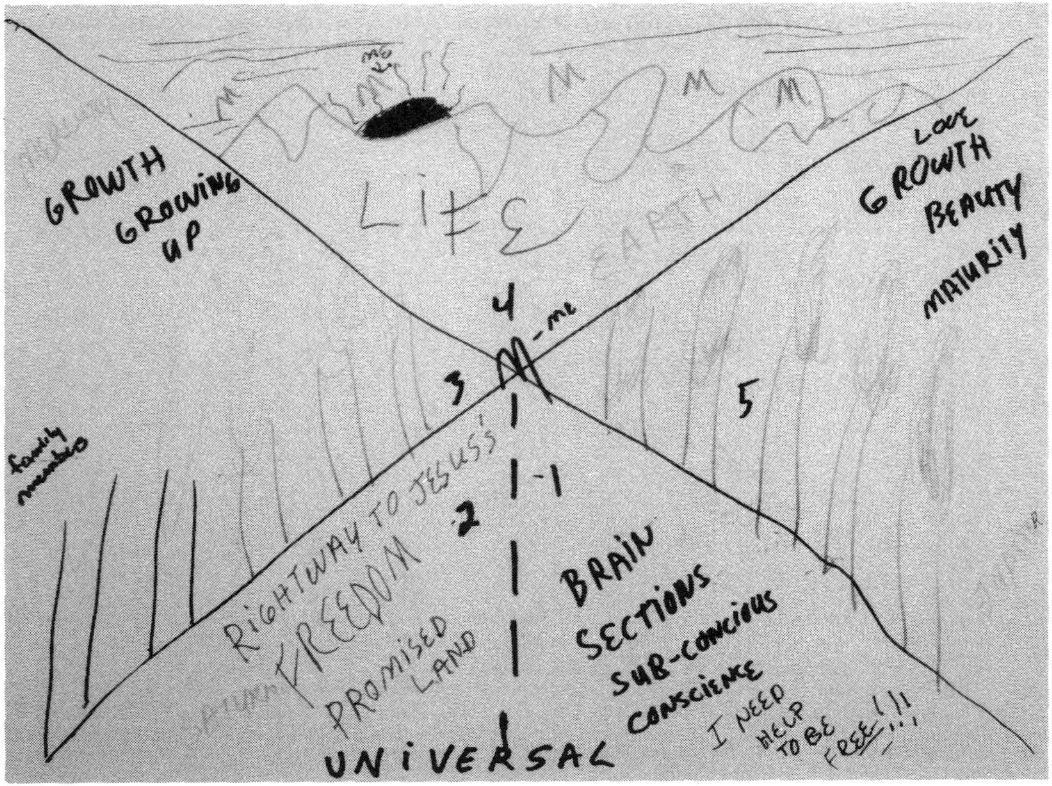

me
LIFE
EARTH
GROWTH
GROWING UP
LOVE
GROWTH
BEAUTY
MATURITY
4
me
3
5
family members
RIGHTWAY TO JESUS'S
FREEDOM
PROMISED LAND
2
-1
BRAIN
SECTIONS
SUB-CONCIOUS
CONSCIENCE
I NEED HELP TO BE FREE!!!
UNIVERSAL

her descent, Susan is stuck in a dark wood, having lost the way. She knows the power of the lower regions, the archaic world, and she knows she needs "help to be free!!!" She draws on Christian thought as an assist (lower left) even as she feels the weight of Saturn, associated with depression and a heavy spirit. Without ever having heard of the collective unconscious, Susan still labels this deep part of herself as "universal." The forest on the left contains "family members" (who were generally supportive). Her astrological associations range from the potential happiness traditionally associated with Jupiter, to the help of the trickster Mercurius.

We see on the one hand Susan's enmeshment in the archaic world of adolescent lethargy, magnified a hundredfold by her psychotic break, and on the other hand the resources available for "growth" and "maturity." The upper quadrant represents her future: "ME," the sun peeking over distant mountains intimating the length and rigor of the journey as well as the promise of transformative travel. The other M-shapes felt to her like herself but also like birds, suggesting the spirit's liberation, the freeing of the iron butterfly.

In her spontaneous drawings Susan was able to mythopoeically depict her dilemma and her journey. She felt terribly stuck, but that she could label these pieces suggests there were clusters of conscious energy just below the surface that could work to assimilate and integrate her split-off parts. Over those mountains the sun shines, like the wisdom of the individuated soul.

Susan was lost in the dark wood, but an inner process was at work, a process that ultimately led to her release and successful reentry into her family and school. In her childlike drawings we see the death-rebirth cycle and the hero's journey. As she carries the universal, and has visited that place where dreams and visions originate, so her very personal images speak to us all. Susan is not making myth; myth is making her. Her task is the same as ours—to make such myth conscious so that we can muster the energy to cooperate with the mysterious teleology of the soul. Those who stand in conscious relationship to such depth images, who apprehend the great mystery they embody, have found meaning no matter how impoverished their outer life may be.

Eating the Sun

The second patient, a boy, was also seventeen. He was born to a navy family and spent his entire childhood on different bases around the world. While his family was posted in Europe he began to experience hallucinations that terrified him. For example, he would see his father killed horribly in a motorcycle accident, or his mother sexually assaulted. Near the base where he lived it was possible to purchase hashish, so like Susan he briefly utilized this drug to defend against these terrible invasions. For some time it was thought that his increasingly bizarre behavior was the result of drug use.

When he was being taken to a military hospital in Frankfurt a voice told him to fly. He leaped off a second-floor stairwell and landed unharmed on the main concourse. After he was hospitalized it was discerned that his experiments with drugs were secondary and not primary causes of his disorganized thinking.

Terry, as we shall call him, was the son of an officer who had fled to the navy as a youth to get away from home. His girl friend became pregnant at eighteen and they lived an itinerant life via the navy. The anger the father carried from his own childhood turmoil came out in alcohol abuse and verbal and occasionally physical abuse of Terry. The mother was sweet, co-dependent and passively seductive. Terry often found himself torn between the two. While he loved and idealized his father, he also experienced his father's self-hatred as oppressive. His hallucinations about his father's death expressed what he could not afford to make conscious. Similarly, the safe, sweet harbor in the family was the mother, who was not only refuge to the emerging adolescent but his secret love as well. The implications of this potential Oedipal drama were too much for conscious assimilation and so they split off and returned as fantasy material.

Terry also readily agreed to do some drawings. The degree of his disturbance went far deeper than Susan's, so his drawings were more eerie and he usually lacked the capacity to talk about them coherently. Often his speech was a form of "word salad" and his visions cosmic in character. He visited other planets and listened in on the gods; his fantasies had a kind of "Star Wars" scope. Of the many drawings he did, one in particular, reproduced opposite, struck me as illustrating his dilemma, his

psychic process and the archetypal character of his experience. The colored original is impressive for its drama and its capacity to touch something in the viewer.

In examining this drawing we must bear in mind that our interests are not aesthetic as such. The more naive and spontaneous the drawing, the more we are allowed to observe the unconscious process in all its immediacy. Joseph Campbell has reminded us of what such mythwork consists:

> [One] must understand that the fragmentary signs and signals signify that [the] patient, totally out of touch with rationally oriented manners of thought and communication, is trying to establish some kind of contact. Interpreted from this point of view, a schizophrenic breakdown is an inward and backward journey to recover something missed or lost, and to restore, thereby, a vital balance. So let the voyager go. He has tipped over and is sinking, perhaps drowning; yet, as in the old legend of Gilgamesh and his long, deep dive to the bottom of the cosmic sea to pluck the watercress of immortality, there is the one green value of his life down there. Don't cut him off from it; help him through.[123]

Upon being asked simply to draw what he was feeling, "where you are now," Terry drew quickly, seemingly without thought. He stepped back and was pleased with his drawing. With greater coherence than usual, he described the animal figure on the left (orange in the original) as a "lizard-iguana-dragon" that was "traveling through time and space." The "sunlight-stricken dragon," he said, will travel through space and "eat the sun," which he identified with the purple, spinning mass at the lower right. Then it will die and "come alive again bright and orange."

The sun, he said, is going into eclipse and has whirling sunspots. Immediately above the sun is an inverted spider watching events. The configuration (yellow) to the right of the "dragon" represents "fall, yellow, winter, sunlight-stricken leaves." The elongated figure at the top right (green) is "a cobra with a prematurely open mouth." The shape to its left is "a pineapple with scab or open vein or blister marks." (These are direct quotes, though not the normal parlance of a teen-ager.) Then he stopped suddenly, put his hand to his mouth and said he had forgotten something important. He had forgotten to draw a half-moon directly behind the

---

123 *Myths To Live By*, p. 209.

dragon (which he then drew in pencil), out of which the dragon had come. The moon, he said, "gives a shit, and doesn't give a shit. It just hangs there."

It is not possible to go into all the motifs in this drawing. But to recall that the young man was suspended between an angry and aggressive father, constantly challenging him to "grow up and be a man," and a passive and seductive mother upon whom he was emotionally dependent, is to see that this drawing does illustrate the family drama and the youth's dilemma.

Terry identified himself with the dragon. Historically the sun has been associated with the Sky God, the Pater Familias, representing solar consciousness, the logos principle. Notice, however, the repeated words "sunlight-stricken." The force of the sun—the too-muchness of the father, whose anger was projected onto the child—had been too great. The pressure to be a man was a Saturnian burden that had profoundly wounded the child.

Without tribal elders to initiate the child with love and wisdom, the youth has nowhere to go in this strange world called manhood, no place he wishes to visit. At the same time, he cannot stay in the bosom of the mother, for to linger there is to perish, to abandon the hero's journey.[124] The sun represents powerful energy that can fructify, bring forth life, consciousness and the divine, but too much of it can wither and destroy what is tender and needing support.

The moon is the embodiment of the unconscious, maternal, waxing and waning in twenty-eight-day cycles, source of all, harbor of respite and siren call to regression. As we have seen in the myth of the eternal return, the sea of eros may give birth but may also cause drowning in "nostalgia" (etymologically, "pain for home"). The moon's silvery sensibility represents intuitive consciousness, while the sun's rays stand for rationalism.

The dragon figure with which Terry identified is a creature of elemental force. Its origins are clearly tied to the mother, and yet Terry is father-bound. To survive he is obliged to escaped the gravitational pull of the mother complex and somehow destroy the negativity experienced in the

---

[124] See my *Under Saturn's Shadow*, especially chaps. 2 ("Dragon Dread") and 4 ("Father Hunger"), for discussion on how men lacking tribal rites of passage become caught in this no-man's-land.

father complex. (Mother and father, as well as being real persons, are internalized as charged energies, complexes, behind which are the archetypes of Mother and Father). The father must die—as Terry's hallucinations suggest—without the person being hurt; that is, Terry must depotentiate the father complex without attacking his biological father. Hence his task is to "eat the sun"—assimilate the negativity, die unto the old ego identity and be reborn as his own person.

The spider is associated with the mother; here it is inverted, suggesting that its energies may be used for the heroic encounter. The cobra also is related to the mother, as is the pineapple, a recurrent symbol of hospitality and homecoming. It is hard for the youth to muster the energies necessary to take on the power of the sun, hence all these split-off components suggest the ubiquity of the mother complex. Still the dragon has immense power.

The motion of the dragon from left to right is the movement out of the unconscious toward greater consciousness. The spiral down to consume the sun, which will "come alive again," is another familiar archetypal pattern, the uroboros, often symbolized by the serpent-dragon eating its own tail. This symbol is found repeatedly in all ancient cultures, East and West; it is the death-rebirth motif, inspired no doubt by the ability of the serpent to shed its skin and grow another. The literature on the serpent as symbol of death and rebirth, as psychopomp and agent of archetypal process (think of the entwined serpents on the staff of the caduceus, the physician's emblem), is widespread. Like all archetypal images it is ambivalent because it seeks to express the diverse sides of any issue. The serpent-dragon can encircle, crush, consume, or heal, lead and transform.[125]

The image of the dragon as a symbol for that archaic inertia which must be overcome is found in the myths of the ancient Chinese, the Phoenicians, Saxons and many others. Apollo, Cadmus, Perseus, Siegfried, Saints George and Michael, are all heroes who overthrow the tyranny of the dragon, associated with all that is powerful, chthonic and regressive. Equally, the serpent-dragon is part of the great cycle of death and rebirth. In the Aztec creation story, for example, the plumed serpent-God wounds

---

[125] See ibid., pp. 38-39, for the fear men have projected onto the serpent precisely because of the depths to which it calls.

himself and gives humankind his blood that they might live. Various gnostic drawings illustrate the presence of the serpent-dragon as the agent of rebirth. There are many myths in which the hero is reborn from within the bowels of the monster—the Greek Jason, Vishnu of Hindu myth and Jonah of Hebrew myth. Each employs the mythologem of rebirth from that which first destroys.

Such an amplificatory summary only begins to trace the rich resonance of the archetypal motif of the dragon as a recurrent symbol. But what does this amplification suggest, and how is it helpful to one who would treat a youth in grave distress?

First of all, the ubiquity of these symbols confirms that there is a richly resonant unconscious life that expresses itself through images, and that each appearance continues the timeless drama of the psyche. When we know that the emergence of the dragon out of the lunar, maternal depths and the subsequent devouring of the solar, paternal sun-god is a myth found in ancient China, fifteenth-century Java, medieval European alchemy, and many other locales and times, then we realize that Terry, like Susan, was not making myth—myth was making him. Because of the radical collapse of the ego, the center that cannot hold, he is living on a mythic plane.

Terry, conceived and wounded by two specific parents, has his own journey of individuation. Nonetheless he joins the long parade of humans on the journey that is incumbent on each of us. We are reminded by the Koran, "Do you think that you shall enter the Garden of Bliss without such trials as came to those who passed away before you?"[126]

We carry this journey in our bones and are destined for it no matter how fate or conscious choice deflects or drives us. Terry's personal and archetypal task is to shake loose from the seductive depths of the unconscious, symbolically destroy the Saturnian Sun-Father, and die unto the sanctuary of childhood. This most ancient of images, incarnating the power of destruction and renewal, lives in Terry's psyche, swishes its ancient tail and breathes fire.

We have seen in these drawings the imaginative logos of souls in what

---

[126] Cited in Joseph Campbell, *The Power of Myth*, p. xvii.

Karl Jaspers termed "boundary situations."[127] Both Susan and Terry were setting out on the first great passage, leaving overt dependence on parents for the provisionality of an untried personality of their own. Neither were helped by their culture, for there were no meaningful rites of passage or wise elders to assist their transit. Both suffered a radical enervation of the ability of the ego to integrate the meaning of their experience into a coherent sense of self. Yet in their drawings we see that the deepest processes of the psyche are dynamic and autonomous, both inspiring and leading the person's quest for wholeness.

In the drawings of Susan and Terry we have visited familiar territory. We have seen the two great mythic motifs: the cycle of sacrifice-death-rebirth, and the hero's journey out of the regressive powers of nature, through the dark woods toward differentiation and individuation. How could it be that these children becoming adults, unlettered and untutored in the old stories, could fashion such images? The only answer is that the same psyche that served our ancestors still serves us. It spontaneously generates such images to activate our energy, guide it and give it meaning. If we have forgotten them, they course within nonetheless. As Rilke notes in his seventh "Duino Elegy":

> Nowhere, beloved, can world exist but within.
> Life passes in transformation.[128]

So the transformative energies move whether we know them or not. How much more meaningful might life be if we could know such stories, our stories, and align our will and our energy with them?

---

[127] *Philosophy and the World*, p. 24.
[128] *Duino Elegies*, p. 61.

4

Tracking the Gods

On the desk before me is a book called *Encyclopedia of the Gods,* by Michael Jordan. Over 2,500 deities are described, ranging from A-a, a Mesopotamian sun goddess, and A'as, a Hittite god of wisdom, through Ignerssuak, an Eskimo sea god, and Yahweh, Hebraic creator god, to Zurvan, Persian god of time and fate.

It seems there is an abundance of gods who have appeared, grown luminous and then receded through the aeons. As we recall from earlier chapters, the mysterious energy that drives the cosmos enters the husk of a concept or belief, abides awhile and then departs. The Immortal Ones, it would seem, are quite mortal. Such a thought, which even a cursory knowledge of history obliges, is disturbing to the believer.

It is no accident that the fundamentalist, right-wing portion of the institutionally religious spectrum has grown since World War Two, while the mainstream Western denominations have declined in number and sociopolitical influence. Speaking to the Guild of Pastoral Psychology in London in 1939, Jung noted that large numbers of people had lost a meaningful connection with the great institutions of Church and Crown. As the ego10 is not comfortable with ambiguity, many had drifted toward the prevailing ideologies of the thirties, notably Marxism and fascism. Those for whom such ideologies did not offer a home, said Jung, internalized their existential angst as neuroses.[129]

After World War Two, with the further decline of the powers of church and state, many drifted into the net of secular ideologies—materialism, hedonism, narcissism—and others joined institutions that could resolve the psychological tensions by declaring dogmatic certainties. When one American president went so far as to aver that America suffered a spiritual malaise, he was attacked by critics for injecting too much self-doubt into the body politic. He was replaced for eight years by a Hollywood actor

---

[129] See "The Symbolic Life," *The Symbolic Life,* CW 18.

who promulgated such sentiments as "America rides tall in the saddle again" while others were "the Evil Empire." The old black and white values were resurgent.

So terrified are the right-wing masses by ambiguity, self-examination and cultural diversity that they lobby fiercely for their agenda and have a political impact far in excess of their numbers or their claim on popular attitudes. Beneath this activity lie fanaticism and fearfulness. This need to insist on the rightness of one's values, and coerce one's neighbor to similar values, only arises when one is afflicted by the demon of doubt. In times of personal or cultural crisis, the strength and maturity to bear the tension of opposites, which is the surest test of sanity, are gravely weakened. To have hundreds, thousands, gather in a rally to trumpet their ideology is not religion, though it has great religious import. The god named as personal confidant by a television evangelist is not God but a cultural or personal artifact. Such reification of the God-imago, as we have seen, is either naive or idolatrous.

There is an equal naivete in those who think they live without the gods, who affirm the sundry delights of secularism or disdain the theologies of their childhood. Jung has written to this point:

> We think we can congratulate ourselves on having already reached such a pinnacle of clarity, imagining that we have left all these phantasmal gods far behind. But what we have left behind are only verbal spectres, not the psychic facts that were responsible for the birth of the gods. We are still as much possessed by autonomous psychic contents as if they were Olympians. Today they are called phobias, obsessions, and so forth; in a word, neurotic symptoms. The gods have become diseases; Zeus no longer rules Olympus but rather the solar plexus, and produces curious specimens for the doctor's consulting room, or disorders the brains of politicians and journalists who unwittingly let loose psychic epidemics on the world.[130]

So that is where they went—storm-shaker Zeus, Wotan the berserker, Aphrodite of the foamy birth. The energy that once invested these figures migrated into the unconscious, only to spring forth anew in the neuroses and pathologies of modernism. This is why Jung also said that a neurosis

---

[130] "Commentary on 'The Secret of the Golden Flower,' " *Alchemical Studies*, CW 13, par. 54.

is like a neglected god, for the principles the gods once embodied have been neglected or repressed and thus reemerge symptomatically.

If we are spiritually sensitive we can read the ciphers of our time. We can see the angst beneath the fervent worship not of the god but of the husk. We can see the thirty-five million who annually trek to Atlantic City casinos as pilgrims in search of a missing Grail, a momentary connection, a transient transcendence of the banality of everyday life. We can see in the sundry addictions of our time, be they to substances or relationships, the fevered drive to connect with the Other. In speaking of such incarnations of psychic life, in saying they are "religious," we are not speaking metaphysically but psychologically. As Jung wrote in 1955 to Pastor Walter Bernet, "I speak of the *God-image and not of God* because it is quite beyond me to say anything about God at all."[131]

Much confusion ensued over Jung's use of the term God-image (or God-imago). Marie-Louise von Franz puts the matter succinctly:

> Every human being has at the bottom of his psyche a divine spark, a part of the divinity which Jung calls the Self. But then all the theologians jumped down his throat. Critics on the theological side, whether rabbis or ministers or priests always say: You turn religion into something which is only psychological. But if we have in our psyche the image of god as an active center, then we should honor the psyche as the highest thing on earth.[132]

A similar confusion surrounds the use of the word Self (capital S) to denote the archetype of meaning and regulating center of the psyche. In German *Das Selbst* is a far more embracing concept than the closer identification of self with ego in English.[133] Its province is body and mind and spirit, and its *telos* is the fullest possible realization of the organism. Just as Immanuel Kant observed two centuries ago that we can never know absolute reality, never plumb the "thing-in-itself," so we can only experience the world through the structures of the psyche. We can, therefore, only know the gods as psychic events, for psychic events, that is, internalized

---

[131] *Letters,* vol. 2, p. 260.

[132] *Alchemical Active Imagination,* p. 53.

[133] In English editions of Jung's *Collected Works* the self as archetype is not capitalized; however most Jungian writers now use Self in order to distinguish it from the mundane ego-self.

experiences, are all we can ever know. Far from demeaning the idea of the divine, or elevating the human, this is a simple, common-sense recognition of the limits of human cognition and verification on the one hand, and the absolute reality of the inner world on the other. This psychoid character of reality was underlined by Jung in a 1951 letter to Heinrich Boltze:

> God: an inner experience, not discussable as such but impressive. Psychic experience has two sources: the outer world and the unconscious. *All immediate experience is psychic.* There is physically transmitted (outer world) experience and inner (spiritual) experience. The one is as valid as the other. God is not a *statistical* truth, hence it is just as stupid to try to prove the existence of God as to deny Him. . . .
>
> People speak of *belief* when they have lost *knowledge.* Belief and disbelief in God are mere surrogates. The naive primitive *doesn't believe, he knows,* because the inner experience rightly means as much to him as the outer. He still has no theology and hasn't yet let himself be befuddled by boobytrap concepts.[134]

Take a moment to contrast Jung's humility before the unknown, his respect for the absolute separateness of the Other and his spiritual strength to sustain ambiguity, with the "certainties," the solipsistic bolts of Thor hurled from ecclesiastical pulpits. Perhaps the vital precondition to religious life ought to be the acknowledgment of the primacy of inner life, the arena in which the God-imago is activated and lives. When the gods are not experienced within, their imagos perforce will be projected outward. Such images, Jung wrote,

> have a high degree of autonomy, which does not disappear when the manifest images change. . . . Our consciousness only imagines that it has lost its gods; in reality they are still there and it only needs a certain general condition in order to bring them back in full force.[135]

When such psychic contents are repressed or slip back into the unconscious, they gather energy and spring forth in events, in affective states or in projections onto charismatic figures or institutions. Jung's 1936 essay "Wotan" illustrates how a one-sided rationalism and technological genius, cut off from the instinctual roots of the German spirit, broke forth in the

---

[134] *Letters,* vol. 2, p. 4.
[135] Ibid., p. 593.

collective disease of fascism.[136]

As we recall the woman mentioned earlier who dreamt of bearing the Christ from her own womb,[137] we realize that such psychic reality is present in all things, but ill-discerned. Those who seek to hold to the uniqueness of their own metaphors, denigrating their neighbor's, are in fact severing their theology from the mysterious roots that first gave it life. In his 1952 letter to Dorothee Hoch, Jung put the matter forcefully:

> The insistence on the uniqueness of Christianity, which . . . doesn't even allow it a mythological status conditioned by history, [renders] the gospel . . . unreal; all possible points of contact with human understanding are abolished, and it is made thoroughly implausible and unworthy of belief. . . . and empties . . . the churches. . . . It is very *convenient* because then the clergyman doesn't have to bother about whether the congregation understand the gospel or not but can comfortably go on preaching at them as before. Educated people . . . would be much more readily convinced of the meaning of the gospel if it were shown them that the myth was always there to a greater or lesser degree, and moreover is actually present in archetypal form in every individual. Then people would understand where, in spite of its having been artificially screened off by the theologians, the gospel really touches them and what it is talking about. Without this link the Jesus legend remains a mere wonder story, and is understood as little more than a fairytale that merely serves to entertain.[138]

A religious tradition severed from its archetypal roots, its mythologic grounding, becomes a set of concepts or rituals without depth. Such a religion is greatly at risk for it lacks the power to stir the soul. Rather than rest everything on the uniqueness of a religion, one might better argue for the particular ways in which it taps the same mythic sources that undergird every other religion. Granting each person the right to his or her own myth or metaphor is the best antidote to bigotry.

The Mystery We Call God

In one of the letters he wrote from a concentration camp, Pastor Dietrich Bonhoeffer suggested that the word *God* should not be used for a century

---

[136] *Civilization in Transition,* CW 10.

[137] Above, p. 59.

[138] *Letters,* vol. 2, p. 75.

because it had become so encrusted with previous associations as to have lost its power to summon up religious experience.[139] Various theologians in recent years have noted the severing of mind and body in Pauline theology, the price of self-estrangement paid by believers for centuries, the denigration of women and homosexuals, and the loss of contact with the telluric mysteries of earth and soul. As Naomi Goldenberg asserts:

> All deities—all goddesses and gods—have to be understood as forces within nature and human beings, within the stuff of life. A male figure who pretends to transcend women, sex, and earthly delight cannot bring life into the world—he can only represent death.[140]

Similarly, trying to stuff all the positive attributes into a single god, excluding those that are contradictory or embarrassing, has created quite a shadow for most theologies. At least the polytheistic religions did not have to worry about contradictions; there was a god to represent every force and value. They did not have a shadow problem, for the gods were understood intuitively as the enlarged expressions of all things human.

In antiquity, as communities migrated, the gods often put off their former attire, donned local garments, even changed their names to the local epithets. But the principles they embodied did not change; regardless of nomenclature, the same divine, that is mythic, principles were being acknowledged. Whether her name be Hera, Juno, Isis, Sophia or Mary, the Great Mother is present. In a letter to Pastor Fritz Pfafflin in 1935, Jung writes:

> What the unconscious is trying to bring you is not something absolutely different from Christianity, but rather a deepening of Christian symbolism and a revivification of the foundations upon which Christianity as well as other great religions are built.[141]

By ignoring or denying their so-called pagan sources, modern religions cut themselves off from their archetypal ground.

Perhaps it is useful, then, to define a god from a mythic perspective as *something that is intimated by, and present in, the affectively charged im-*

---

[139] *Letters and Papers from Prison,* p. 152.
[140] *Changing of the Gods,* p. 105.
[141] *Letters,* vol. 1, p. 192.

age that emerges from an experience in depth, an archetypal encounter.

The image itself is not the god, but the image is so affectively charged as to reconnect us to the depth experience. What the ultimate mysteries are, of course, we cannot say. But as we experience them they activate the God-imago in our own psyche. Just as the personal parent, for good or for ill, activates the parental imago within each of us, so archetypal encounters activate the God-imago. Analogously, an outer event may activate a resonant response in our unconscious in the form of a stirring dream. We would not confuse the dream with the outer event. In fact, we would understand the dream as ours. But the images of the dream partake of both something from outside and something that is very much in us—and also of something still more mysterious.

Just as the dream image intimates and is present in the experience but is not the event itself, so too a god is experienced as an image that hovers somewhere between outer and inner but can only be experienced inwardly. To consider a dream as a psychic event is not to denigrate it; rather it is to say that it has a true phenomenological reality. To say that the experience of God, or the gods, is a psychological event is also to say that it has a true phenomenological reality. That reality may not look like that of the theologian or the evangelist, but it is the phenomenological experience of the individual. Without that immediacy, one has not had a religious experience, no matter how much one affirms belief in a credo or participates in a social ritual. As Jung explained in a letter to Valentine Brooke in 1959:

> When I say that I don't need to believe in God because I "know," I mean I know of the existence of God-images in general and in particular. I know it is a matter of universal experience and, in so far as I am no exception, I know that I have such experience also, which I call "God."[142]

In other words, Jung uses the word *God* to mediate the outer and inner worlds. As this is a felt experience, it is real for him. As it is real for him, the idea of God is beyond theology, beyond creed or ritual, and certainly beyond understanding.

Anyone who works with the reality of the psyche, the reality of soul, encounters such presences and is awed by them. In his talk on "The Sym-

---

[142] Ibid., vol. 2, p. 522.

bolic Life," Jung reminded his audience that our primal ancestors knew well the presence of such a God-imago. Their gods were within, had a resting place in their psyche, and the world around was richly appareled with the divine. Asked whether our effort to understand rationally was doomed, or actually harmful, Jung replied:

> Only when the intellect breaks away from that symbolic observance. When the intellect does not serve the symbolic life it is the devil; it makes you neurotic.[143]

So, when mind destroys the affective charge of the image, or denigrates the power of the nonrational inherent in the phenomenological experience, the God-image dies. This surely is what Nietzsche meant a hundred years ago when he declared in "Thus Spake Zarathustra" that God is dead and we have killed him. Nietzsche, the Basel professor, knew as well as the simplest peasant that when the intellect severs the symbolic image from the affective charge, or when the institution crushes the spontaneity of the imago, then the god dies. Thus, the most reverent of attitudes is the one that periodically smashes images which have become idols, and humbly confesses its ignorance, readying itself to receive the archetype anew.

As Blaise Pascal observed in the seventeenth century, "Every religion which does not affirm that God is hidden is not true."[144] Only the hidden god is the true god, for the god who can be known has already become an artifact of conscious culture and is in the process of disappearing. In Rilke's words:

> Gods—we project them first in audacious images
> which constricting fate destroys for us again.
> But they are the Immortals
> who in the end will hear us.[145]

To track the gods is to see them at work within our sudden panics, our projections, our rages, all the complexes that possess us, exactly as the ancients described—Medea slaying her children, Oedipus rending his eyes, the heavy hand of the gods on a family through the generations.

---

[143] *The Symbolic Life,* CW 18, par. 665.
[144] *Pensées,* no. 584, p. 161.
[145] *Sonnets to Orpheus,* part 2, no. 24 (author's translation).

I am reminded of an analysand, Hans-Peter, whose father was an illiterate farmer who immigrated to a new part of his country. His lack of education, his dialect and his poverty served to set him off from others. The father was only able to express himself through the language of senseless, indiscriminate violence. He possessed a handgun and was feared by his neighbors. He was in frequent altercations, some of them physical. Hans-Peter was repeatedly beaten, as were his two older brothers. Only the fourth son, who contracted "the divine disease," epilepsy, was spared abuse and entered adult life without significant problems of adjustment or abiding rage against life in general. The two eldest brothers were trapped in the violence and also acted it out.

Hans-Peter was caught between the two worlds. Hovering thus, he internalized most of the violence and suffered recurrent bouts of depression. Even so, he had had his share of fights. While in the army he rebelled against authority and was confined to a correctional battalion. He would not answer letters from creditors or pay traffic tickets, but managed to obtain a degree in engineering. In the course of his analysis he came to see how he was unconsciously living out the curse of the gods. His father and his whole blood-line had been driven by Ares-Mars. When he truly grasped that he was laboring under the weight of this god, he could also see that he had choices. His father had been driven by the unknown god, so it possessed him demonically, but Hans-Peter had other gods who could come into play as well. In order to become himself he at last understood that the task fate had presented him was to break the spell the mad god held over his family.

In using metaphors such as the possession of a family by Ares-Mars, we are acknowledging how a part of the psyche can split off and be projected onto others or gain sufficient autonomy to rise up and take charge of the individual. It is important not to confuse the Self with the idea of God. To identify oneself with a split-off energy can lead to a dangerous inflation, to the *Fuehrer* complex for example. The psyche is the matrix in which the god can incarnate, whether conscious or not, but to identify with that incarnation is madness. The task of the ego is to dialogue with the god, that is, with the energy the God-imago is incarnating. In a letter to Pastor Damour in 1932 Jung explains:

The human psyche and the psychic background are boundlessly underestimated, as though God spoke to man exclusively through the radio, the newspapers, or through sermons. God has never spoke to man except in and through the psyche, and the psyche understands it and we experience it as something psychic. Anyone who calls that psychologism is denying the eye that beholds the sun.[146]

Tracking the gods means paying feeling attention to the incarnation of the archetypal images, whether they occur in the venue of dream, somatic complaint or political event. Images that spring from the head only are, like certain progeny of Zeus, deformed; they are merely ideologies, doomed to partiality and rapid decay, however much they may initially capture the ego's enthusiasms.

When we understand that the human psyche is the matrix for the experience of the gods, the forge and smithy of divinity, we learn, as Augustine wrote, that "that which thou seekest is near and already coming to meet thee."[147] Jung added:

All ages before us have believed in gods in some form or other. Only an unparalleled impoverishment of symbolism could enable us to rediscover the gods as psychic factors, that is, as archetypes of the unconscious. . . . All this would be quite superfluous in an age or culture that possessed symbols.[148]

Once perceived as ambulant beings, the gods are now seen as dramatizations of cosmic principles, principles we embody as well, for we are not alien to them. This encounter with the gods cannot be willed; it is a delusion that the ego can summon up the depths at will.

Returning to the source, that is, to the reality of the psyche, frequently obliges the individual to forsake the comforts and certainties of group-think. Such a person must leave behind the collective values of the tribe. Even more, coming into proximity with the source may require the death of the God-images that served one in the past. (Recall the woman who said to me, "My individuation began the day my god died.") Often a great

---

[146] *Letters,* vol. 1, p. 98.
[147] *Confessions,* p. 186. Compare this with Pascal's thought: "Console thyself, thou wouldst not seek me, if thou hadst not found me." *(Pensées,* no. 553, p. 149)
[148] "Archetypes of the Collective Unconscious," *The Archetypes and the Collective Unconscious,* CW 9i, par. 50.

loneliness comes with the loss of the old certainty, causing many to herd together for protection from the reality of the living gods. In fact, one may observe, without cynicism, that the task of many religious institutions has been to protect its flock from religious experience! If one is not to surrender to the easy assurances of the herd, then, as Jung said, "he has to go on the Quest; then he has to find out what his soul says; then he has to go through the solitude of a land that is not created."[149]

What an enormous opening this is—to find out what one's soul has to say! In that commitment to the reality of the godly journey, one's life is flooded with dignity and purpose however arduous the road. One finds there is a fundamental buoyancy to the cosmos after all. Jung suggests,

> When you are in the darkness you take the next thing, and that is a dream. And you can be sure that the dream is your nearest friend; the dream is the friend of those who are not guided anymore by the traditional truth and in consequence are isolated.[150]

If the crisis of the age is religious, and the crisis of the individual is neurosis, then the task is not to throw the baby out with the bath water. Erich Fromm rightly cautions us:

> The question is not religion or not, but which kind of religion, whether it is one furthering man's development, the unfolding of his specifically human powers, or one paralyzing them. . . . We can interpret neurosis as a private form of religion, more specifically, as a regression to primitive forms of religion conflicting with officially recognized patterns of religious thought.[151]

To ignore this question of the gods, or to relativize them, is to muck deeper into the miasma of modernism. To ignore the gods is to guarantee that they will exact some form of revenge in the privacy of neurosis or the horrific theater of history. The imperative of soul calls the individual, like it or not. On the one hand are the various forms of totalitarian thought, theological and political, and on the other the easy relativism of a culture that has lost its moorings. The burden of meaning, as we noted in the first chapter, has almost wholly been turned over to secular institutions. If we

---

[149] "The Symbolic Life, *The Symbolic Life,* CW 18, par. 673.
[150] Ibid., par. 674.
[151] *Psychoanalysis and Religion,* pp. 26-27.

may say that even in a neurosis one may find the tracks of the wounded, violated or neglected gods, then we may also say that the divine is everywhere, the trace of the gods evident, however secularized and profaned.

Out of this confusion a few things are clear. First, the encounter with depth, whatever form it may take, occasions a mediating image. That image is not itself divine, but for a time it does hold divine energy. Secondly, we cannot fix that energy in an image we institutionalize and worship. Such energy has a life of its own and will depart, appear elsewhere or go underground. Thirdly, the burden of meaning has fallen inescapably upon the individual. No one can live that journey for anyone else. Those who consign the journey, out of their understandable fear and loneliness, have just consigned their lives away. What is required is the acceptance of loneliness and suffering, the mustering of patience and courage, and faithful attentiveness to the movements of psyche.

As difficult as this journey may be, it brings the individual back to the gods. Just when we thought them gone, by tracking the movement of soul within us and within history, we experience them moving in our midst again. We cannot know that mystery, yet we can follow it. As Jung noted at the end of his 1937 lectures at Yale University:

> No one can know-what the ultimate things are. We must therefore take them as we experience them. And if such experience helps to make life healthier, more beautiful, more complete and more satisfactory to yourself and to those you love, you may safely say: "This was the grace of God."[152]

Adrift on the Cosmic Sea

In the last chapter of *The Middle Passage* I suggested that often one found oneself as though on a storm-wracked ship. Looking back we see no port to which we can return; ahead there is only the endless horizon. There is no crew, no captain; we alone must decide whether to go below and fall asleep, hoping the ship will founder on some pleasant shore, or grab the wheel and sail on. This metaphor also occurred to John Berryman:

> Whether the moorings are invisible
> or gone, we said we could not tell.

---

[152] "Psychology and Religion," *Psychology and Religion,* par. 167.

But argument held one thing sure
That none of us that night could well endure:
The ship is locked with fog, no man aboard
Can see what he's moving toward,
There is little food, less love, no sleep,
The sea is dark and we are told it's deep.

Where is an officer who knows this coast? . . .
            Who knows how,
With what fidelity his voice heard now
Could shout directions from the ocean's floor?
Traditional characters no more
Their learned simple parts rehearse,
But bed them down at last from the time's curse.[153]

The old authorities have lost their power and the maps are missing. The time is cursed and those adrift on the cosmic sea are in peril. Nonetheless, they must sail on.

The myths that have evolved among the peoples of the world, addressing the varied questions, constitute an immense treasure. One can spend a lifetime reading and reflecting on such abundance. Yet the more one reads, the more one begins to circle back upon old trails, old questions. The guises of local time and place may vary, but the patterns are there and await our recognition.

A metaphoric schema which permits us to see the patterns amid the plethora of mythic materials is what I have called "the cosmic drama." If one were to take all the myths of all peoples of all times and combine them, one would have, in effect, the human story in all its permutations. Moreover, such a story would be highly dramatic for it is not static but a process, a dialectical movement, a universal, timeless rhythm. In no single myth would we see the whole story, or all the patterns, but each would dramatize at least one motif of the cosmic drama. Comprehending this overall narrative would allow us to identify where each mythic motif, including those from our own traditions, fits into the larger scheme of things; moreover, we would also be able to see where our individual lives enter into this timeless drama. Especially because of the spiritual sterility of

---

[153] "Conversation," *The Dispossessed,* p. 42.

our time, it is enormously healing to learn that we in fact participate in a larger rhythm. The meaning of our lives derives from the journey of individuation, which is intimately interwoven into the cosmic drama.

The concept of the cosmic drama assists us in identifying the recurrent patterns, the motive and movement that informs each myth, and how those suprahistorical patterns are also replicated in the life of the individual. The origins and ends of the great drama are shrouded in mystery, to be sure, but each person is called to serve that mystery. By becoming oneself as fully as possible (which is what Jung means by individuation), one serves the larger purposes of history. This is not a form of narcissism, for it frequently calls for us to walk a path other than the one the ego would have chosen. Often it is a humbling experience. Yet then the individual serves the mystery by undertaking his or her part of the cosmic task.

The message of the cosmic drama is familiar to us in the phrase "ontogeny recapitulates philogeny." The individual being carries the genetic code and the archetypal patterning. Therefore when we look at the cosmic drama we must see it at two levels simultaneously—as the story of the species and the story of the individual. And, like any drama, it has a structure. To my mind there are four acts: chaos, creation, separation and going home.

1. Chaos

What lies before being, before beginning? What caused First Cause? Our finite intelligence falters, mislays the Ariadne-thread back through the labyrinth of imaginal time and ends in chaos, in the primal soup, the cosmic sea, the chthonic mud and slime, the roiling billows of start-stuff. Each people has its metaphor of this state before, before consciousness and therefore memory, so it could not be described. It is a metaphor of the time when the earth was without form and humans nonexistent. In the life of the individual this act corresponds to the fetal state where we float timelessly through the unconscious sea, wafting on the great tidal currents of blood and protein.

2. Creation

At some instant in the before-beginning it happens, it moves. But what is "it," the great catalyst? We do not know, so we are driven to find images, to wrest from the unknown a semblance of sense, a metaphor to carry over from the unknown to the knowable world. The various tribes find metaphors that touch them emotionally. For one tribe a god speaks. For another, earth and sky copulate. Great careening forces collide, and being is begun.

Whatever the metaphor, something occurs to set the process moving. The cosmic egg cracks. The uroboros splits into opposites. The void conceives and bears fruit. From these dramatic renderings of the mystery of birth, two great forces are set in motion in history and in the individual. We may call them the forces of *eros* and *logos*. Eros is the power that adheres, seeks connection, recombines and synthesizes. Logos is the power which separates, differentiates, leaves behind and develops. Eros provides the drive to reconnect with others, with nature, with the gods. Logos is the drive to differentiate at the cellular level and then in the attainment and development of consciousness.

3. Separation

For something to be, it must differentiate itself. I am me because I am not you, nor am I the tree over there. Polarities are necessary for definition. Light and dark, day and night, male and female, earth and sky, sea and firmament, moist and dry, life and death, and so on. The infant who floats in the cosmic sea of mother's womb has no identity, for it is not over-against an Other. Separation from the mother is painful. Thrust violently into a world of blinding light, shattering sound, gravity and strangeness, the newborn's wound is enormous. Birth is a loss of connection, a fall from grace, a descent into mortality. Yet without that separation a person would not exist, for one exists only in one's separateness.

The polarity of opposites is critical to the birth of a human. We share our instinctual life with other animals, but the experience of that critical polarity makes consciousness possible—to awaken from the instinctual slumber, to become aware and capable of processing, remembering, intending. It is the paradoxical loss of umbilical connection, to the instinctual world for the tribe, and to the mother for the infant, that occasions consciousness and the capacity to be human. Out of polarity comes consciousness, out of consciousness comes the capacity for choice, out of the capacity for choice comes moral sensibility, and out of moral sensibility arises maturity.

Each tribal unit had at some point in its history to make the great leap from instinctual gratification to sublimation. (One sees the intimations of such great moves, for example, in the later books of the Bible, Job in particular, and in Euripides' *Oresteia.*) Our creaturely comrades move to the surge of instinctual rhythms. They gather food before winter, sleep, copulate, move out of harm's way, but do not name themselves, comprehend abstractions like money or justice, do not become neurotic, do not love or slaughter their neighbor on behalf of a slogan. All of these things require a reflecting consciousness.

The growth of consciousness is a spiraling process. With each turn of the loop, one moves further from the instinctual life. With each move the tribe or the individual gains greater and greater control over the instincts and the natural world, but suffers a concomitant loss. This gap between instinctual life and consciousness is called neurosis, a necessary price for evolution. The more fully evolved the consciousness, the higher the burden of responsibility. Growing and maturing as a society and as a person means spiraling toward ever more consciousness, reexperiencing one's separateness and circling upward again.

4. Going home

Precisely the separation that furthers consciousness also occasions great suffering. The further one moves from the instinctual life, the further one is from home and the more one suffers. All tribes have their myth of the Golden Age, the Happy Isles, the edenic time before suffering and consciousness. They were not there, but surely their great ancestors, the First Ones, were. Perhaps it is the genetic memory in us all that occasions this nostalgia. If it is true that our ancestors lived in an age of gold, supplanted by the age of silver and bronze, and that we live in an age of iron, so it is also true that the gods walked the earth then and spoke directly to our ancestors from burning bushes, great sea spouts and the earth itself. No, we are not there now, but we would like to be.

However desirous it may seem from a distance, being adult, conscious and responsible is onerous. It is so demanding that periodically all of us would like to drop the burden and retreat to a simpler life. Through the years at least three recurrent patterns have evolved in every culture in every age and in the life of most individuals. Each pattern represents, whether one is conscious of it or not, a backing off from the rigor of the journey, the ubiquitous angst on the high seas. They are infantilism, chemical regression and ideological dependency.

Infantilism

Being an adult has virtually nothing to do with age or size, but rather with the level of consciousness and the level of personal responsibility to which one has evolved. Whining about fate, accidents of birth or parenting, or one's moment in history, are examples of infantilism. Expecting someone else to take care of us is another. The two great delusions hardest for humans to shake are the fantasy of the "magical Other," the person who is going to enter our life and make it work, make it meaningful and painless, and the fantasy of "immortality," wherein the mortal thread which links us all to the human condition applies only to others. Living a life of narcissistic preoccupation, the search for immediate gratification and the systematic avoidance of pain and responsibility for self and others are still other common patterns of infantility. Sadly, these characteristics apply to great masses of humans in the modern era. So many creature comforts, so much vicarious, voyeuristic living, so much flight from the abyss over which one daily walks.

Chemical regression

Various chemical substances have been ingested from the beginning of time to provide access to sacred vision. From the wine-mad celebrants of Dionysus, to the wine-blood of Christ, to the peyote-ingesting Indians of New Mexico, chemical substances have been employed in the holding container of ritual in order to connect with the transcendent. But far more commonly, food, drugs, tobacco and alcohol have been used to dull the pain of psychological adulthood and stupefy the sense of separation. The more a culture loses its mythic moorings, the more prone it is to substance abuse. Such substances provide momentary surcease from spiritual pain, a hedge against the harshness of the journey, but the price paid is the level of consciousness necessary for growth.

The reflexive resort to substances pulls one back to sleep with the

Mother. It is a form of anxiety management. As the level of mythic disconnection rises, so does the level of angst. Through the regressive move, a momentary connection is experienced and one feels the intimation of wholeness through the Other. That sense can only be sustained for a short period and therefore must be repeated often. This is the birth of addictive behavior, whether the search for connection is through the guise of food, chemicals or the warm flesh of another. So great is the pain of separation that one hears the goal is to "feel no pain," "get wasted," "stoned," "obliterated." As everyone has addictive behaviors, that is, reflexive responses to unacceptable levels of anxiety, so we all fall into patterns that attenuate the evolutionary spiral of consciousness.

Ideological dependency

The third common way to avoid the burden of consciousness is to relinquish it to the group or Great Leader. We have seen entire nations relinquish their individual consciousness and moral values, following charismatic leaders on holy rampages. From Jonestown to evangelical fundamentalism to the blandishments of commercials, the lure of group-think is all too evident. Every ideology is based on some kind of idea, perhaps even a good one. But any idea that is universalized to apply to all, that suffers no doubt or internal criticism, that polarizes people, becomes demonic. Any ideology—religious, political, even psychological—that would simplify the world's complexities in order to make the individual more comfortable is demonic. Those who offer easy answers do not understand the questions. Staying within an ideology, rather than growing through the necessary suffering of life, is another version of regression.

Each of us may periodically regress through one or more of the above patterns, so great is the rigor and duration of the journey. But an awareness of the breadth, diversity and imperative of the cosmic drama requires that we also respond to the mythic call that echoes through the corridors of history and in the marrow of our bones.

All we have to offer in face of the great regressive powers within and without is the willingness to undertake the journey. The awareness of duality, of conflict, is painful, but choosing to pursue one's individuation is the only adult choice, the only way to live one's life to the fullest and at the same time serve the larger mystery. This is a choice made not once only; it must be renewed every day in the face of the demons of fear, doubt and lethargy.

If we step back and look at the tangled skein of human history we can see the cosmic drama in its full majesty. There are many losses, many regressions, many wrong paths, but the ineluctable surge of soul can be clearly seen at work through time and through the individual. As Jung said, "Each individual is a new experiment of life in her ever-changing moods, and an attempt at a new solution."[154] Jung's myth of individuation is a myth for an age without myth. The metaphor of the cosmic drama is a way to locate the soul's journey when all the other compasses are missing.

We are only a tiny fragment of history, but we carry the promise of it all. As travelers in an age which has lost its myth, our individuation task is a conspicuous note in a great song that has been sung from the beginning.

---

[154] "Analytical Psychology and Education," *The Development of Personality,* CW 17, par. 173.

5
The Gods Astir:
A Mythic Interlude

All the stories of this spinning earth cycle forth from the recurrent themes of love and death, power and pride. Such motifs are as old as civilization and as recent as last night's dream or this morning's business conference.

As we have seen, the gods are the dynamic energies that rise out of archetypal encounters. They leave their traces in luminous images, but the images are not the gods; they are the temporary containers of that divine energy. How natural it is for the human to grasp at the image in order to hold the energy, possess the god. This impulse manifests as idolatry and its wicked step-child, ideology. Nothing drives the godly energy away faster than our desire to fix it in its evanescent course. And the human is left to lament, "O you lost god! You unending Trace!"[155]

We cannot possess the gods, although a great number of priests and theologians have labored to do so. Rather it is the divine energies that contain us. Our language recalls this heritage; we may feel enthusiasm *(entheos,* the god within) and ecstasy *(ek-stasis,* literally to stand outside oneself, to be transported), just as we may be jovial or saturnine. These energies possess a portion of the psyche and cause us to do things beyond the ego's power to understand or control.

While the energies are divine, the experience of the gods is perforce an intrapsychic event, since the psyche is the only arena in which we can experience any reality. Accordingly, despite the ego's despotic desires, the psyche is a multiplicity of energies occupying now this locus and now that. Some of these loci have sufficient charge to be called complexes. Beneath every personal complex lies its archetypal component, the energized pattern which is a universal. If madness can be seen as the possession of consciousness by one of these fragments—possession by a mad god, to speak metaphorically—then sanity must surely grow through consistent

---

[155] Rainer Maria Rilke, *Sonnets to Orpheus,* part 1, no. 26.

dialogue with these psychic components.

Our ancestors knew this intuitively. They could see how an Oedipus, reportedly the best and the brightest, could overthrow reason and restraint, even advanced knowledge, to murder a man he resembled and who was old enough to be his father. They could see how a mad mother called Medea could slay her own children. Or they could know first hand those Medusan encounters with evil so chilling as to freeze the soul into immobility. These stories seemed at worst silly and at best histrionic when first we encountered them as bored school children. But we have lived a bit longer now and have experienced our encounters with the godly powers; we may even feel a shiver when we meet them. We now know our psyche to be less a flashlight in a cave, as the ego would have it, than a kaleidoscopic activation of energies here, and there, and somewhere else.

The figures that animated ancient mythology move through our souls, trouble sleep and sometimes act out in unsettling ways. The scenarios of ancient script are now visible in the plots we have been enacting, albeit in a thousand thousand variations, and we knew it not. To read such stories with sensitivity and openness is to link ourselves up again with the timeless zones of the soul. When such images touch something within us, the gods have returned and are moving in their invisible but numinous ways. In Rilke's words:

> Once again let it be your morning, gods.
> We keep repeating. You alone are source.
> With you the world arises, and your dawn
> gleams on each crack and crevice of our failure.[156]

So, love and death, the *Liebestod,* the old, old story, gods and humans intermingled, poised on the cliffs of time, staring into the cavernous depths of soul.

Liebestod Variations

One can take any myth and discern behind its regional coloration the universal pattern. This is why Aristotle suggested that myth was more revealing than history. One can become caught in the particularity of history, but

---

[156] "Now It Is Time That the Gods Came Walking Out," in *The Selected Poetry of Rainer Maria Rilke,* p. 277.

in the myth the timeless pattern is manifest. To illustrate this we shall examine some lesser-known figures of Greek myth and how the patterns they personify are reflected in the modern world.

Admetus and Alcestis

As a form of community service plea-bargain, Apollo is obliged to serve Admetus, king of Pherae, after his slaying of the Cyclopes. As Admetus is a kind master, Apollo is grateful and offers a favor in return. Because Admetus is destined to die young he requests a sort of stay of execution. Apollo seeks to cajole the Fates with wine but can only win a surrogate sentence—Admetus can live longer if someone will agree to take his place at the previously scheduled hour.

Understandably, the line of volunteers for this substitution is not long. Even when he visits his parents he receives short shrift. College, apparently, they could afford, but they had just purchased a condo in Boca Raton and were looking forward to enjoying the golden years themselves. Only his wife, Alcestis, agrees to take his place. (This story was cast as an opera by Gluck, called *Alcestis,* following the plot line of Euripides' play in 438 B.C.E.) The nobility of Alcestis's sacrifice moves even the godly ones and they subsequently return her to life. While the play is obviously a paean to her nobility, Admetus is obliged in his grief to confront his cowardice and selfishness.

One has to wonder what kind of life would be possible to this couple after events of such magnitude. Would love heal, or would memory torment? On the one hand, the natural fearfulness of Admetus becomes monstrous when he is willing to sacrifice another to prolong his own life. On the other hand, the willingness of Alcestis to relinquish her life to save the man she loves is remarkable.

I recall a couple I saw some years ago. The husband, William, was a corporate executive, a good-hearted man but lacking in any deep sense of himself. He in fact was very anxious about death and, having little sense of self, was clearly identified with the trappings of power and affluence. He drove the latest and most expensive of cars, visited the plushest of spas and surrounded himself with possessions. Any bodily symptom sent him into an anxiety attack. He dyed his hair and had surgical tucks here and there. His chief support and emotional caretaker, his Alcestis, was his wife Adele. His emotional development lagged far behind his chronological age, so his anima development was dependent on the care and feeding of his mate. She mediated his fears, assuaged his anxieties and continuously bolstered his ego.

Her devotion to him might have seemed admirable in another time where gender roles were sufficient for self-definition. But we live in a age where each is expected to develop, to individuate. As William dumped his emotional development onto his Alcestis, so Adele lived her role instead of her life. When she died in an auto accident, William was inconsolable. He died of a heart attack a few months later. It is often the case that one spouse quickly dies after the other; their unlived life comes back to haunt them. Adele died not knowing herself as a separate being; William died as emptily as he had lived.

As the structural anthropologists remind us, each version of the myth is true, for each mythologem is polyfaceted. The nobility of tragic, ennobling sacrifice in one version of the myth becomes the pathos of the unlived life in another. Admetus and Alcestis live on in William and Adele.

Philemon and Baucis

How different is the story of Philemon and Baucis, as one learns from Ovid's *Metamorphoses*. It seems that Zeus and Hermes once decided to disguise themselves as humans and to travel among the mortals to see how they were living. At last they came to a meager hut in Phrygia where they were welcomed by an elderly couple, Philemon and Baucis.

Poor as they are, the two press their only food and wine on the gods in genuine warmth and sharing. The gods are impressed by this generosity of soul and reveal their divine nature. They explain how moved they are, given the ungraciousness of most humans they had met along the way. They transform the modest hut into a marble temple and ask the couple what most they would like to receive. Philemon and Baucis reply that they would like to be permitted to serve the gods in this temple as long as they live, and not be separated from each other in life or death. When their time comes, they die peacefully. Philemon becomes an oak and Baucis a lime tree, their boughs entwined, together forever.

It was as an undergraduate in the early sixties that I first read *The Story of Philosophy* by Will Durant. Even then I was touched by the epigraph

Will wrote himself and dedicated to his wife Ariel:

> Grow strong, my comrade . . . that you may stand
> Unshaken when I fall; that I may know
> The shattered fragments of my song will come
> At last to finer melody in you;
> That I may tell my heart that you begin
> Where passing, I leave off, and fathom more.[157]

In these words, written in the mid-twenties, the husband sees his mortality clearly, affirms his devotion to his wife and to their partnership, and expresses the fervent belief that after his own death she will be able to deepen the work they undertook together. In fact, Will and Ariel Durant formed a life-long marital partnership and a life-long professional collaboration (most notably on the eleven-volume series, *The Story of Civilization*). Ariel died first, Will a matter of days later. Like Philemon and Baucis, they had been blessed by the gods for their generous souls—they had each other for companions and produced a body of work that survives as a temple long after them.

It seems that Philemon and Baucis lived through more than one marriage, and that the gods blessed more than one couple.

Dido and Aeneas

Virgil's *Aeneid*, the Latin epic, sought to do for the Roman Empire what Homer had done for Hellas. Most of the text is devoted to the trials of Aeneas, heroic survivor of Troy, who would go on to found the new civilization of Italia (or Latium). But even as one's imagination is fired by his struggles, the heart is stopped by his love affair with Dido in Carthage.

When Aeneas and Dido fall passionately in love (this is an Italian epic, after all), Mercurius is sent to remind Aeneas of his journey and that he may not tarry in Carthage. Dido pleads with Aeneas to stay with her, but offering a series of rationalizations he sails off to his imperial destiny.

While the meaning of the *Aeneid* has often been interpreted as the necessary sacrifice of the pleasure principle, or of private motive, to serve the reality principle, the collective good, one cannot but sympathize with the pain of the abandoned Dido whose young man sails off to war and will

---

[157] *The Story of Philosophy,* p. v.

never return. Distraught and bitter, she slays herself with his sword. Much later in the journey Aeneas makes a descent into the underworld. Among the many shades he encounters there is his beloved Dido. Once again he offers rational explanations but she turns away without uttering a word. Seldom has silence spoken so thunderously.

Many years ago, I was a colleague of Virginia, an intellectually gifted woman who was a history professor. She frightened the undergraduates and most of her colleagues as well. She was perceived as rigid and narrow; she used her intellect and verbal acumen to cut people off, maneuver them to her point of view and shame them. Everyone respected her scholarship, but no one liked her, myself included. When she reached the then obligatory retirement age, we all breathed a sigh of relief.

During the years I had known her, I had never had a truly personal conversation with Virginia, nor had anyone else I knew. But when the time came for her to go into a retirement home I volunteered to help move boxes she had carefully packed. I took my two-year-old daughter Taryn with me, and after the move we sat exhausted on the floor playing together. Suddenly Virginia said, "I would have given anything if my father had sat on the floor and played with me."

It was the first time I had heard anything of her inner world. We got to talking and I gingerly asked about her life, not knowing when she would cut me off. "I was in love once," she said. "He went off to the war and never came back." That was all she would say, but I could tell that she felt betrayed by the two men she had given her trust to. My heart softened; I knew then what I should have known all along, that here was simply another wounded soul. From that brief opening we developed a sort of friendship that continued through correspondence when I moved away.

Even now I cannot help but think of the forsaken Dido when I envision Virginia standing forlornly as her Aeneas sails off to do battle. When he did not return, Virginia, like Dido, killed something in herself. Her relations with others remained estranged, cold and bitter for the next four decades. She lived her life by turning away, silently, disdainfully. Protecting herself from further wounding, she ended her emotional life and lived in the underworld, dead before dying.

All versions of the myth are true.

Glaucus

Glaucus was the son of Sisyphus, he of the never-ending boulder, and the father of Bellerophon. Glaucus was also the owner of race horses. So proud of them was he, and so anxious to maintain them forever at peak performance, that he refused to breed them lest their strength be weakened. He also fed them human flesh.

Jung noted that a neurosis is like an offended god, that is, an archetypal principle which has been wounded or neglected. In not allowing his horses to breed, to follow their natural function, Glaucus had offended Aphrodite. On the occasion of funeral games for the fallen Pelias, Aphrodite decides to punish Glaucus for his pride and vanity. During the night she leads the horses out of their restraints and allows them to drink at a well sacred to her, around which grow herbs that will render the beasts uncontrollable. The next day Glaucus loses control of his horses; he is caught up in the reins and dragged about the stadium. In the end he lies on the ground sorely wounded and his horses eat him alive.

Frederick was a cleric married to a woman whom many mistook for his mother. Their natural life together was entirely replaced by the claims of his churchly office. They functioned well in the world as a team, but their marriage was without intimacy. As a result Aphrodite was wounded. By night Frederick would roam the streets of his medium-sized city wearing longshoreman's clothing, looking for boys and street hustlers to pick up. By day he was a powerful orator, administrator, politician; at night the horses of instinct fed on those herbs that bring madness. His life was out of control.

Predictably, Frederick's world came crashing down. The story made all the newspapers and he had to leave his church and his city. In the end, he was undone not by his sexual predilection, but by the arrogance of office that protected his wound and allowed no introspection, and by the vanity fed by his worldly success. In diverting the course of his nature, he fell victim to his nature's revenge. The gods will not be mocked.

Idomeneus

One of the many heroic captains who sailed his vessel and led his hosts to the siege of Troy was Idomeneus, valiant voyager and at the forefront of the action, according to Homer.

On the perilous voyage home after the topless towers of Ilium had fallen, a ship-wrecking gale attacks the fleet. Idomeneus vows that if he is allowed to survive he will sacrifice to Poseidon the first living thing he finds. That proves to be his son, who has hurried to the shore to welcome his father home. In some versions of the story he slays his son, in others he seeks to evade his promise, but in either case a plague breaks out in the land and he is driven into exile by his disaffected people.

The motif of the person who impulsively, selfishly, makes a deal with the devil occurs repeatedly in myth and legend. "The Girl With No Hands," a Grimm fairy tale, comes to mind. In that story the father fatuously bargains with the Evil One, promising to give up the object behind his house, which turns out to be his daughter. What the devil represents mythically is the archetypal encounter with the shadow, with our own darkest, meanest impulses. We have met the enemy and he is us, as the saying goes.

How many parents have offered up their children on the altar of their unrealized ambitions? How often does the drive for success cause the adult to sacrifice the child? Or, even more common, how often does the sea-surge of ambition, or pride, or vanity, demand the sacrifice of the child within that adult, the wounding of that which kept the world fresh and full of enlivening possibilities? All of us, at some time, on some surf-wracked shore, have lived out the Idomeneus in us.

All versions of the myth are true.

Marsyas

Earlier in this book I confessed to a "Faustian" phase of life, a time when I thought I could pile up bricks of knowledge until a veritable tower might result, whereby the gods could be seen in all their luminosity. Well, we know what happened to the Tower of Babel.

Much later, while training at the Jung Institute in Zürich, I spent many an afternoon wandering the halls of the Kunsthaus, the municipal art gallery. On more than one occasion I found myself circling back to stand before a certain antique statue. I recall thinking of Freud standing before Michelangelo's *Moses,* and how it represented the pulls and tears in Freud's own psyche, how he was playing out the timeless conflict between id and superego. When I began dreaming of my antique statue, I knew it had some special meaning for me. It had ceased to have a merely intellectual appeal; I had been touched more deeply than I knew.

I did some research on the statue and its theme, and learned that what I was so taken with was a Roman copy of an earlier Greek statue of the satyr Marsyas. According to Pindar, the goddess Athena had invented the flute. Marsyas was fascinated by the instrument and insisted on playing it even though he risked her displeasure. In time, he played the flute so well that people gathered to hear him and applaud. Some even suggested that he played better than the great Apollo. Marsyas began to believe his press reports and offered no demurral.

This was a bad career move on his part. It does not pay to take on the gods, who represent the dramatization not only of ultimacy but of limitations as well. It is the human flaw, the *hamartia*, of hubris, that causes us to forget our limitations in the face of ultimacy.

A contest ensued, a shoot-out at the Delphic Corral, with the victor offered unlimited revenge on the loser. The smart money was rightly on Apollo, who won. He tied Marsyas to a tree and flayed him alive. The particular statue in the Kunsthaus depicted Marsyas hanging, twisted on a tree, much in the conventional pose of Jesus on the cross or St. Sebastian pierced by arrows.

In meditating on this antique stone and why it had so fascinated me, I recalled that the word fascinate comes from Latin *fascinare,* to enchant, bewitch, that is, to cast a spell. Thus the outer image was stirring something within me, something essentially unconscious but also numinous. Then I realized that I was undergoing a form of ego-crucifixion by the gods. That is what Zürich meant for me; that is what depth analysis is for. In my youth I had made a Faustian pact with the dark forces: knowledge equals power. I had put many blocks on the tower, but it had to tumble.

We often find at midlife that the ego-structure we have assembled over the years, even—or perhaps especially—when successful in the outer world, constitutes a "false self" whose maintenance can only occasion further and further self-estrangement. Massive energy has gone into the construction of this false self, which now hangs precariously over an abyss. It all has to tumble for new life to emerge. But the transition is fraught with anxiety, depression and huge uncertainty.

The Fates, or my own unconscious, kept leading me back to stand before Marsyas, just as they had colluded to bring me to my knees, to Zürich and a confrontation with the Self. I could not have been touched by the outer image, and the myth, if they did not mirror my own myth. Unwittingly, I had taken on the gods. I deserved to be humbled, brought down, flayed, in order to be open to the parts of my soul that had been neglected by my inflated ego. I had to learn that I did not know anything. I had to learn a daily humility, that the mystery was infinitely greater than I could know. Only a youth would have thought otherwise. So, the mystery that haunts that hunk of stone reached out to me and brought me closer to the gods after all, but in a fashion no ego could have contrived.

We have touched here on only a few of the lesser known myths to illustrate a point. The range and richness of mythic motifs is virtually endless; it moves across centuries and across cultures and, if one reads carefully, may even be seen between the lines of today's newspaper.

Each myth is the dramatization of those invisible energies that flow through the universe and, for awhile, inhabit us. Collectively, they tell the whole human story and the cosmic drama. Each one expresses a fragment of the whole, part of a chapter. Each of us lives one verse or another, moving to rhythms deeper than consciousness can plumb. Let us be grateful for these images even as we are grateful for our dreams; they tell us in visible form of the invisible at work in history and in us.

When we have an emotional response to an age-old story or motif, we have a handle then on the invisible world as it affects us personally. As I was moved by the image and the fate of Marsyas, incarnated in a piece of stone over 2,000 years old, so I was able to discern something deeper afoot in my life in the twentieth century. Reading myths with the mind's eye, with imaginal receptivity, tells us that the gods really did not go away. They just changed their form and now stir us in new ways.

6
Mystic Chords of Memory

The Better Angels of Our Nature

Jungian psychology takes its place in the context of modernism and the loss of mythic connection. Freud, Jung and the other pioneers of "the talking cure" responded to the erosion of institutional values on the one hand and the limitations of the new sciences on the other. They slowly came to discern that there were wounds to the soul which neither agency could treat. It would be wrong, however, to consider depth psychology as a "soul science." Perhaps it is best described by the German word *Seelesorger*, "soul carer."

Caring for the soul, attending the deep wound to one's meaning, is what depth psychology is about. Most schools of modern psychology represents a failure of nerve to address the soul. Behavioral, cognitive and pharmacological approaches have much to contribute, but they remain superficial because they do not attend the wounds of the soul. The depth psychologist is attuned to symptoms, even to symptom relief, but the question is rather what these symptoms mean, what soul-wounds are manifesting themselves.

Therein lies the vital role of myth; myth delineates the movement of soul. Sometimes the analyst can recognize a mythologem in a person's dream and discern the character of the wounding and the likely course of healing. "What myth," one asks, "is this person living?"

Jung has defined neurosis as living within too narrow a personal myth. When, in the second decade of this century, he asked himself, "What is my myth?" he could not answer the question. Thus he began an intensive self-exploration, working with his dreams, developing the technique called active imagination, and undertaking the descent that either destroys or heals. He dialogued with the images that rose to meet him and from that encounter those split-off energies were partly integrated and enlarged the field of his conscious life. This, ultimately, is the role of therapy, meditation, active imagination and dream interpretation—to assist one in living the conscious, reflective life. When we can adjust our outer life to accord with those emergent, spontaneous images of inner life, we feel a deep resonance and healing. According to the gnostic gospel of Thomas, Jesus said, "If you bring forth what is within you, what you bring forth will save you. If you do not bring forth what is within you, what you do not bring forth will destroy you."[158]

The loss of myth consciousness and our search for a new myth has even reached the ears of the politicians. In 1994, Vaclav Havel, president of the Czech Republic, came to Philadelphia to receive the Freedom Medal (given the previous year to Mandela and DeKlerk). In his address, he noted that our age was going through a time of enormous upheaval:

> The distinguishing features of such a transition are a mixing and blending of cultures, and a plurality . . . . of intellectual and spiritual worlds. These are periods when all consistent value systems collapse, when cultures distant in time and space are discovered or rediscovered. . . . [For us] the artificial world order of the past decades has collapsed and a new, more just order has not yet emerged. The central political task of the final years of this century, then, is the creation of a new model of coexistence among the various cultures, peoples, races and religious spheres within a single interconnected civilization.[159]

So far, this sounds like any politician's preamble to some new vision of order that would be imposed from above, the standard ploy of ideologues. But instead Havel went on to argue for two principles (in addition to the fundamental respect for human rights and freedoms), namely the "anthropic cosmological principle" and the "Gaia hypothesis." The former notes that

> from the countless possible courses of its evolution, the universe took the only one that enabled life to emerge. This is not yet proof that the aim of the universe has always been that it should one day see itself through our eyes. But how else can this matter be explained?

---

[158] Elaine Pagels, *The Gnostic Gospels,* p. 152.

[159] This and the several excerpts following are from the transcript of the speech titled "Address of the President of the Czech Republic, His Excellency Vaclav Havel, On the Occasion of the Liberty Medal Ceremony, Philadelphia, July 4, 1994."

Clearly this principle is very close to the notion of our necessary participation in the cosmic drama, as discussed in the previous chapter. The Gaia hypothesis avers that

> the dense network of mutual interactions between the organic and inorganic portions of the Earth's surface form a single system, a kind of mega-organism, a living planet—Gaia—named after an ancient goddess who is recognizable as an archetype of the Earth Mother in perhaps all religions. According to the Gaia hypothesis we are parts of a greater whole.

Havel believes these two principles are necessary to the new world consciousness:

> Both remind us, in modern language, of what we have long suspected, of what we have long projected into our forgotten myths and what perhaps has always lain dormant within us as archetypes . . . . the awareness that we are not here alone nor for ourselves alone, but that we are an integral part of higher mysterious entities against whom it is not advisable to blaspheme. This forgotten awareness is encoded in all religions.

Is it possible that a politician could be speaking of goddesses, of archetypes, of myths encoded in our species? Yes, but Vaclav Havel is no ordinary politician. He is a poet and playwright too, a humanist. Havel represents the enlightened, reflective spirit of our time. He concluded his speech with the hope for transcendence,

> as a deeply and joyously experienced need to be in harmony even with what we ourselves are not, what we do not understand, what seems distant from us in time and space, but with which we are nevertheless mysteriously linked because, together with us, all this constitutes a single world. Transcendence is the only real alternative to extinction.

Transcendence means to be lifted out of the isolation of ego consciousness and the desolation of existential abandonment that characterizes the soul of the modern. It means to feel connected to a spiritual order larger than oneself.

At the same time as one places provisional hope in such leaders as Havel, so we must, individually, do our own work. Jung repeatedly noted that the single best thing one could do for the world was to integrate our own shadow, to lift off the world's shoulders our personal part of the burden. As I pointed out in *The Middle Passage,* echoing Rousseau, all are born free, yet everywhere are in chains. The natural being, the child, is whole but powerless and dependent. Thus the child must adapt his or her natural intent to the power of the environment, especially the family of origin, thereby adopting a provisional sense of self and Other, and a set of strategies for interaction. This assemblage of behaviors has as its central purpose the moderation of anxiety.

It is only when this provisional self repeatedly collides with the natural, instinctual self which pulsates from below, that people become conscious of the split we call neurosis. One might characterize the whole first half of life as a gigantic mistake, as necessary as it is unavoidable. The task of the second half of life is to recover from that mistake, to move from the adapted self to the authentic self insofar as we may approach it. To leave the known, adapted self, with all its flaws and pain is an awesome thing, for it has brought us this far and we fear the great unknowing that succeeds it. The middle passage consists of leaving home psychologically, a task we thought already accomplished by the earlier physical separation. So, even though we suffer within the constraints of the false self, we cling to it desperately.

Again, we must notice how much the situation of the individual replicates the situation of the age, how the neurosis of the individual mirrors the anguished split of the Zeitgeist. As the age has lost its sustaining mythos, so the individual at midlife or at other points of critical choice has lost his or her personal myth. To be between myths is a painful, frightening experience. To suffer our spiritual split so deeply is to experience the deep tension of a civil war. All wars are civil wars; all neuroses are civil wars: different parts of the same whole are estranged and in conflict with each other.

As a child growing up in south-central Illinois I was deeply imbued with the spirit of Abraham Lincoln. My maternal grandmother is buried a hundred yards from him in Springfield; my paternal grandparents are buried twenty feet from his beloved Ann Rutledge in Petersburg, and family legend has it that a great, great grandmother, Elizabeth, was dandled on The Great Railsplitter's knee in New Salem. But one does not have to spring from that place on earth to have been touched by the deep, pervading influence of that wise and melancholic man who traveled from the

Sangamon to the Potomac, whose words moved those from Petersburg, Illinois to Petersburg, Virginia and beyond, a man who truly believed that our terrible Civil War, with its 600,000 dead and 1,000,000 casualties, was the vengeance of a just Jehovah for the sinful slavery of one part of the body politic by another.

On March 4, 1861, with the fratricidal tensions growing ever keener, Lincoln used the occasion of his First Inaugural Address to appeal to the shared history, the transcendent memory, of the revolution and of the common fathers, Washington, Adams, Jefferson and Franklin. Like Vaclav Havel in Independence Hall in Philadelphia, Lincoln sought transcendence, the search for unity through the appeal to the American mythic memory. Here are the last two sentences of his speech:

> Though passion may have strained, it must not break, our bonds of affection. The mystic chords of memory, stretching from every battlefield and patriot grave to every living heart and hearthstone all over this broad land, will yet swell the chorus of the Union when again touched, as surely they will be, by the better angels of our nature. [160]

In examining the nature of a civil war, outer or inner, we are easily tempted to lay blame. In the political sphere it is easy enough to demonize the enemy. In the personal sphere it is easy to stay locked into the secure and known, as Auden suggested, or blame others for why our lives do not seem to work out. The fantasy of the "magical Other," the one who will fix and heal us, make our lives meaningful, or conversely the one who has caused our unhappiness, is the second hardest fantasy to relinquish. (The hardest, recall, is that of personal immortality, that despite all the evidence we will not die.) Such thinking is an abdication of personal responsibility and therefore of personal development. And it is a poor gift to share with another, for the quality of outer relationship can never be any better than the level of consciousness attained in the relationship to ourselves.

We cannot know ourselves fully, or possibly even well, and quite apart from the sundry self-deceptions of the ego, we needs must end with as much perplexity as clarity. Indeed, we stand a better chance of knowing the ocean in its entirety than of fathoming the depths of our own soul. As

---

[160] *Selected Speeches and Writings,* p. 146.

Sir Isaac Newton confessed,

> I do not know what I may appear to the world, but to myself I seem to have been only like a boy playing on the sea-shore, and diverting myself in now and then finding a smoother pebble or a prettier shell than ordinary, whilst the great ocean of truth lay all undiscovered before me.[161]

And Gerard Manley Hopkins added, "O the mind, mind has mountains; cliffs of fall / frightful, sheer, no-man-fathomed."[162]

They dissemble who say that God never gives humans more than they can bear, for the world is full of people destroyed by their own darkness or that of others, as anyone who walks the clinical wards or reads the papers can attest. An analyst friend of mine once said of her unconscious, "There is something in there that wants to destroy me." At the same time we intuitively know there is something in there that wants our healing and our wholeness, and that our hope and sense of purpose derive from it.

I have been drawn to Jungian thought and practice because of two facts. First, it is an attitude toward, and methodology for, working with the soul; and second, it helps me make sense of my life. Yes, it is true that Jungians employ arcane concepts like anima, animus, archetype, complex and the like, for which they are often ridiculed by their psychological brethren, but the whole thrust of Jungian work is to promote the dialogue between ego and Self. Even other psychologists know this, hence many of them go into Jungian analysis.

As children we suffer the wounds of too-muchness or not-enoughness, feeling overwhelmed or abandoned, and wind up adapting our souls to protect our wounds. What a difference it would make in the life of a child, and of the whole world, if the parent could repeatedly, sincerely, say: "You are brought into life by nature having all you need. You have a great force, a great spirit, a great energy within. Trust it, stay in contact with it, and it will always lead you toward what is right for you. Never hurt another person, but always be true to that great inner force and you will never be alone and never without direction."

I have yet to meet a person who ever heard such words, or their vari-

---

[161] *Oxford Dictionary of Quotations,* p. 362.
[162] "No Worst, There Is None," lines 9-10, in *Poems of Gerard Manley Hopkins,* p. 76.

ants, or internalized such a message to guide their journey. One purpose of therapy, then, is to remind each person of that great truth within. By attendance upon symptom as symbol, by dream work and active imagination, we are slowly reconciled, sometimes painfully but always meaningfully, to our own truth. The mythic construct we call the Self is simply a way of incarnating, of talking about, this inner locus of natural purpose.

The central indication of whether a person can make headway in therapy is the ability to internalize, that is, have enough strength to turn inward and face the forces contending there in civil war. If one stays locked in blaming others, or narcissistically seeks a realignment of the environment to render it congenial, then he or she will stay stuck forever in a reflexive response to the outer world, tied to a false self, a maladaptive cluster of strategies that compulsively repeat variants of the original response to life's trauma. For this reason therapy, whether formal or in solitary self-reflection, requires years of listening, regressing, integrating, before recovering a larger relationship to the instinctual self.

Since most modern psychologies emphasize the importance of environment and the modification of behavior, Jungian psychology is a kind of anachronism, for it takes its impetus from the tradition known as essentialism, the hypothesis that there is a given nature from which we have become estranged, but which in its healthful or wounded ways is always present and acting through history. For all the short-term appeal and efficacy of other modernist psychologies and philosophies, I am obliged by practical experience and personal intuition to align myself with the unfashionable essentialist view.

If we are less persuaded by the essentialist arguments of Plato and Western romanticism today, still we sense in our bones the coursing of a deep truth. We are obliged to re-member, to re-cognize, to re-collect. The I Ching describes the "superior man" as one who lives in the house of self-collection, and just so, we are obliged to pull back projections and integrate them.

Many years ago, Milton Rokeach, who wrote *The Three Christs of Ypsilanti* and was president of the American Sociological Society, told me of his return to the small village of his birth in Poland. There was one remaining survivor of the Holocaust. When the Nazis came through they destroyed the local Jewish cemetery and used the gravestone fragments on roadsides and around lakes. That surviving man chose as the work of the rest of his life to find those fragments and to reassemble the graveyard, not only as a memorial to his murdered friends and family, but as a reconstruction of his own myth, a living myth for his present. If he is still living, I imagine that man even now, with this infinite jig-saw puzzle, living out a metaphor that might have animated the stories of a Borges or a Kafka. Surely his heart-breaking, heart-ennobling work is less to create a memorial, however, than to reconstitute his own sense of self. The mystic chords of memory, indeed . . .

But what, then, constitutes the work of soul? What binds us to ourselves, keeps constancy, is dependable? We know that our cells are ever dying and regenerating (though at a slower rate as we age), and that we are not the same eyes, hair, brain matter, viscera we once were. We know with Heraclitus that we cannot step twice into the same stream, for not only does the stream flow on but we are not even the same person the second time. What, then, provides the continuity, gives us a consistent personal myth? Is it the mystic chords of memory?

The surrealist poet Apollinaire observed that memory is "a hunting horn whose sound dies out along the wind."[163] What is remembered, what not? What is accurate, what distorted by the shape-shifting psyche? Perhaps, as the structural anthropologists would have us believe, all versions of the myth are true; all variants of memory are true in that they value what has become crucial to the individual's personal legend.

Just as every myth is polyfaceted and each variant reflects another surface, so memory is a hall of mirrors where our own many faces shine back. When we talk of Dionysus, or Aphrodite, we are obliged to identify *which* Dionysus, *which* Aphrodite, for the tales are myriad and often contradictory. But all are true. As anthropologist Claude Levi-Strauss expressed it, "We do not claim to show how men think in myths, but how myths think themselves in men, and without their knowledge. . . . myths think themselves among themselves."[164] Jung similarly observed: "Man

---

[163] "Hunting Horns," lines 11-12, in Angel Flores, trans., *An Anthology of French Poetry from Nerval to Valery*, p. 252.
[164] *Savage Mind*, p. 97.

does not make his ideas; we could say that man's ideas make him."[165]

Not only do we move to archetypal rhythms, consciously or not, we are also driven by the emotionally charged imagos of our personal history, especially the mother and father complexes. It is apparent that, quite outside the field of consciousness, we serve these ideas and they control our choices. Of course these mythic "ideas" are less concepts in the cognitive sense than emotionally charged energies we are obliged to translate into explicit thoughts if we are ever to make them conscious.

Thus the wound of neglect or abandonment, for instance, occasions a reflexive, phenomenological distrust of the world on the one hand, and a diminished sense of self-worth or personal solidity on the other. Neither conclusion is warranted but results from a flawed reading of the world. Objective reality is lost before the subjective power of primal experience. The mythic idea that "I am unworthy, and can only contract relationships in which that unworthiness is reiterated" is a charged, internalized mythologem of greater power than the fragile entreaties of consciousness. This is why therapy that is truly transformative takes so long. The mere correction of a faulty idea or self-defeating behavior does not reach deeply enough into the traumatically charged and internalized energy. The amendment of such a mythologem as personal unworthiness requires years of emotional releasing and the patient building of an alternative experience of self that is not based on the vagaries of the Other out there, whom one can never control.

What we call a complex is a splinter mythology, an emotionally charged image, an implicit thought or motif, a fragmented world view that binds one to the norms of an earlier experience. The psyche is forever asking the implicit question, "When have I been here before?" The stimulation of the complex activates the historic scenario and contaminates the reality of the present.

Each of us has large amounts of undigested psychic experience stored in the unconscious. When a stimulus activates the personal myth, the energy tied to the primal experience, which was overwhelming perhaps to the child, still has the power to flood the adult. One analysand, after years of

---

[165] "Freud and Jung: Contrasts," *Freud and Psychoanalysis,* CW 4, par. 769.

separation, remained powerless to serve his wife with divorce papers. He was paralyzed by fear, for she evoked the stern, critical parent of his childhood and he could not be a bad boy in her eyes. The incest victim who repeatedly crosses the boundaries of others is contaminating the present through an internalized phenomenological mythos. Just as the psyche is timeless, so myth is timeless and operates in invisible ways.

Two years ago, at an Independence Day celebration at Penn's Landing in Philadelphia, a woman stood enjoying the night-time fireworks. Suddenly she suffered a panic attack and had to rush home. She said of her experience, "I held the outside together, but inside I felt terror." During this same time her ninety-three-year-old mother was dying. She felt shut out from her mother, now as always before. "Mom won't share anything with me, not even her death."

In going through her mother's papers she came across a clipping from 1942. Though her mother was an American citizen, she had emigrated to Russia in the thirties and her daughter was born in Moscow. When the war began, mother and daughter took a long train ride across Siberia to Tokyo where they were briefly imprisoned as enemy nationals. After awhile they were released and sailed for Vancouver. The child remembered that their ship was bombed after it left Tokyo harbor and several were killed although the ship continued to Canada. Her mother, for reasons unknown, had always denied that such an incident had taken place, and the daughter had come to distrust her memory, thinking that perhaps she had recalled a movie or a bad dream. But there, in a yellowed clipping, was the account in a Vancouver newspaper of the bombing of "The Empress of the Orient," just as she remembered.

Confronted with the clipping, the mother still denied the event ever occurred, even though she had saved the clipping herself. The analysand concluded, "My mother would not let me have my own reality." The outer fireworks that initiated her panic replicated the falling bombs of long ago and far away, causing the undifferentiated material to surge forth with all its primal terror. Myth thinks us, as Levi-Strauss would say, or the person's ideas, even those that are unconscious, make the person, as Jung would say. This woman had carried the phenomenological misreading of her world, mediated by the pathology of the mother, all her life; she felt not only unworthy but insubstantial, bereft of her own grounding.

All of us have felt overwhelmed, stupid, embarrassed, when dominated by the force of a splinter myth or complex. Freud once described therapy as after-education or reeducation *(Nacherzieung)*. The word *education* comes from the verb *educe*, to lead out from within; thus therapy entails a drawing forth of that which is already there, timelessly. The capacity of a person to heal, to grow beyond the pernicious invasions of the past, requires the achievement of a psychological adulthood in which one is able to live in the present. Fortunately, the adult can often absorb the emotional charge that was overwhelming to the child, put it into some sort of comparative experiential frame, and assimilate much of its energy. This is why Jung said that we never really solve our problems with life, that is, the core wounds; but we may, if we suffer them through, outgrow much of their toxic contamination of the present.

As we are an assemblage of behaviors, attitudes toward self and others, and charged, reflexive mythologems whose motive and contents are fueled from the past, so we find it difficult to live in the present. The more these charged imagos are unconscious, the stronger the compulsion to analogously repeat the past. The ancients intuited this secret relationship and observed how fate wounds, but the responsibility for one's choices, and therefore for the meaning of one's life, is still one's personal burden. So, again, we recall the classical concept of the *hamartia*, the wounded vision of self and world, the refracting prism of childhood experience through which the adult makes choices that bind him or her to repeat the past in a thousand variations. The piper then to be paid is Fate, with which we collude when we elect to remain ignorant or unconscious.

As of this writing I have presented a workshop on the personal myth in nine different cities in North America. One of the questions I ask to stir reflection and response is, "Where are you stuck in your life?" In not one of these workshops has a single person asked, "What do you mean by that?" Nor has anyone paused very long in starting to write a response. What does this tell us? It tells us that we all know, by now, where our growth has stopped, where the snags in the stream of life are, where we repeatedly get stuck in the reiteration of the "same old, same old." And most of the twelve-step programs aver that we are foremost stuck at the level of denial.

"What you resist will persist."

Setting out on the path of individuation, as easy and as obvious as it may seem, is an awesome task. It obliges leaving home psychologically, leaving behind the old comforts of place or person or ideology. It requires embarking on the journey toward the soul, a journey both joyous and intimidating. Often a cloud of undifferentiated angst seems to block the path.

Angst is formless, free floating, paralytic. If the cloud of unknowing can be converted to specific fears, then often the path opens. What was overwhelming to the child, such as the loss of approval, is internalized as an undifferentiated emotion that is activated in other situations and thereby blocks action and personal integrity. Thus one is caught in the transference phenomenon—the dynamics of past relationships imported into the present. The child's fear of losing the parent's favor is recirculated in adult relationships. The mythologem of the abandoned child—"I cannot live without the other being there for me"—is transferred to the contemporary scene. By making the mythologem conscious, one can achieve a standpoint vis-à-vis the emotionally charged material. The adult may very well be able to risk disfavor today, especially in the light of the need to live a responsible life, and may be able to set the pernicious past aside sufficiently to act appropriately in the present.

The liberation of being in the present is the aim of therapy and of the reflective life. As Thomas Merton argued:

> What can we gain by sailing to the moon if we are not able to cross the abyss that separates us from ourselves? This is the most important of all voyages of discovery, and without it, all the rest are not only useless, but disastrous.[166]

Naturally the old gremlins of fear and lethargy sap the energy necessary for the conscious examination of one's mythos, but if the task is not renewed daily, the whole purpose of evolving life is violated. The Persian poet Rumi observed:

> A king sent you to a country to carry out one special, specific task. You go to the country and you perform a hundred other tasks, but if you have not performed the task you were sent for, it is as if you have performed

---

[166] *Thomas Merton: Spiritual Master,* p. 431.

nothing at all. So man has come into the world for a particular task, and that is his purpose. If he doesn't perform it, he will have done nothing.[167]

As important as the task of individuation is in giving one a chance to operate more and more out of the natural self, and relieve in part the terrible feelings of inauthenticity, so individuation is equally critical to the quality of relationships with others. Hence Jung wrote,

These two things, the immense concentration on one's inner world and the immediate response to the other person, were to me the synthesis of the whole human being. The unrelated human being lacks wholeness, for he can achieve wholeness only through the soul, and the soul cannot exist without its other side, which is always found in a "You."[168]

Individuation and Relationship

In my view there are four principles that are inescapably present in all relationships, intimate and otherwise. They are:

1. One can achieve no higher level of relationship to another than one has achieved in relationship to oneself. Relationships are always implicitly contracted at the level of the psychological evolution of each of the parties. For this reason relationships are frequently rent by heartache and blind conflict as one outgrows the earlier level of the contract or is blocked in the attempt to evolve.

2. What we do not know or cannot face about ourselves, for example the mythologems (complexes) that drive and direct us, is projected onto others. A huge hidden agenda left over from one's childhood is typically projected into the relationship. The partners inevitably suffer the growing discrepancy between these unconscious agendas and the reality of the other, leaving each sad, confused and angry.

3. Power insinuates itself into all relationships. Power itself is neutral; it is the exchange of energy between two parties. But where consciousness is lacking, the level of the power drive becomes a function of the complexes at work and power replaces love. A conflict over power is a symptom of what is working unconsciously in the relationship.

---

[167] *Feeling the Shoulder of the Lion: Poems and Teaching Stories*, p. 21.
[168] "The Psychology of the Transference," *The Practice of Psychotherapy*, CW 16, par. 454.

4. Individuation is not self-indulgent but in fact enhances the quality of the self we bring to the other. We love the other by lifting off him or her the burden of healing us and making our life meaningful. We free the other in proportion to the degree we have freed ourselves. This is surely what Jesus meant when he asked us to love our neighbor as we love ourselves. It is not possible to love the neighbor without the capacity to love oneself first. Thus, the paradox of personal myth is that we frequently impose it upon the other, albeit unconsciously, and relationships falter and fail. Only a greater knowledge of one's myth can enhance the quality of relationship.

Relationships always involve our case history. Yet our history is a fiction, not as it happened but how we construe it. A fiction is not something untrue, any more than myth is untrue; it is something made (Latin *facere*, to make). Our personal mythology, our case history, is a thing made, an emotionally charged narrative with clusters of energy which then relates itself, autonomously, in dreams and in waking life. Our history is not objective reality, whatever that might be, but our mythology, with all its variations, all of which are true. We are at once abused orphan, unworthy friend, heroic voyager, child of our era and more, all outside of time; and, more grandly, we are also the subject, purpose and carrier of an archetypal drama. We will never know who we are any more than Newton could grasp the ocean of truth roaring beside and within him. Still, we cannot abandon the attempt to achieve a deeper relationship to our own myth.

We are living these mythic imagos whether we know them or not, will them or not, suffer them or not. We are therefore obliged to seek a more conscious mythography lest we serve slavishly the iron fates that set all in motion. Robert Calasso expresses our dilemma:

> The mythographer lives in a permanent state of chronological vertigo, which he pretends he wants to resolve. But while on the one table he puts generations and dynasties in order, like some old butler who knows the family history better than his masters, you can be sure that on another table the muddle is getting worse and the thread ever more entangled. No mythographer has ever managed to put his material together in a consistent sequence, yet all set out to impose order. In this, they have been faithful to the myth . . . . [for] myth allows of no system.[169]

---

[169] *The Marriage of Cadmus and Harmony*, p. 281.

The mythographer knows what the therapist knows, that there is no one truth, that all the variants, even contradictory ones, are somehow true. Consider how liberating this is in contrast to fundamentalism, the insistence that my ego-bound, complex-ridden truth is superior to yours. William James, in his epochal work toward the beginning of this century, *The Varieties of Religious Experience,* expressed no discomfort at the plethora of religions in the world. Rather than see them as mutually contradictory, he saw them as variants of the myth, as it were, appealing to a variety of temperaments. The Jungian view of the psyche is that it is polycentric, that it is only the nervousness of the ego that seeks sovereignty over soul. The proper dialogue which enhances individuation is between the ego, central complex of consciousness, and the sundry other complexes supping at the table of soul.

Yet the ego and its anxious henchmen, who are fundamentalists at heart and need security over the complexity of truth, are appalled by this vertiginous dilemma. When we reach out for philosophical assistance we see that metaphysics is long dead, and structuralism, poststructuralism and deconstructionism have passed through as momentary fashions, each undermining the notion that there may be such a thing as truth, or an Archimedean point on which to stand or from which even to survey the terrain. We know that the primary folly imbedded in neurosis is the delusion of the ego that it is in charge, even as its authority is undermined by split-off contents. And it is the folly of psychosis to abandon the ego's precarious position and surrender to the command of the dark gods. Paradoxically, the reason why we pay attention to dreams, for example, is to deconstruct the false sense of reality of a constricted conscious life and to enlarge its perspective, to see the world as that fictive construct the Self does.

What is left to us in the Jungian, post-Kantian world is to employ our constructs as consciously as possible. We are impelled to render our mythic components more consciously, yes, but with the added knowledge that all the variants have a truth, of sorts, and that we juggle fictions when we talk of ego, Self and even the "I" that expresses these thoughts. Wallace Stevens noted this necessary fictive shift, this metaphysical wink, in a poem titled "A High-Toned Old Christian Woman." The poet dialogues with her and concludes that he, the poet, and she, the theologue, are really doing the same thing, making fictions. But the poet remains free in the conscious play of fictions while she is trapped in her idolatrous literalism. He concludes, "This will make widows wince. But fictive things / Wink as they will. Wink most when widows wince."[170]

If we are to chart our own myth, with all its variants, we are obliged to wink frequently, to play with the sundry disguises of the Self, lest we fall into the idolatry of literalism, the psychosis of fundamentalism.

By now, then, we are in more than a bit of muddle, or, as Yeats wrote, "We are locked in / and the key is turned on our uncertainty."[171] Jung once said that the damnable thing about the unconscious is that it is unconscious. As the structuralists would have it, each imago contains its opposite and, though the mind demands resolution, all variants are true. For the deconstructionists, with no signifier there is no signified—all is context. So we are well painted into a corner, If it is true that our relationships with others can never be more conscious than our relationship to ourselves, and if it is true that we do not stand a prayer of ever completely knowing ourselves, then all relationships are doomed to be impaired.

Regrettably, most relationships *are* impaired, some profoundly, whether between parent and child, between groups, between peers or intrapsychically. But wait, all is not lost! A grain or two of honesty will oblige us to admit we are our own worst enemies. For instance, one technique useful in counseling couples is to ask each partner to identify the wounded patterns of his or her history that repeatedly trouble the relationship. By identifying the images within that disturb the outer world, one takes an heroic step toward unburdening the relationship.

If we could diagram our psyches at any given moment they would look roughly like the air traffic controller's screen at O'Hare airport at rush hour. Incoming wide-body complex, departing commuter complex and so on. How difficult, how impossible, is self-knowledge; how difficult, how impossible therefore are relationships. Pessimism reigns, psychological sureties are dashed.

---

[170] "A High-Toned Old Christian Woman," lines 21-22, in Ellman and O'Clair, *Modern Poems,* p. 90.

[171] "The Stare's Nest by My Window," lines 6-7, in *The Collected Poems of W.B. Yeats,* p. 202.

Yet with this salty taste of realism, this pessimism, even this cynicism, we are still stunned from time to time by a secret confession, that we intuit a deep inner truth to which we were close in childhood but only occasionally experience today. This is a truth that runs deep down the marrow of the bones and in familiar feeling states, a truth we may trust if we can hold to it and bring courage to bear in order to live it. From the metaphysical and epistemological debris of modern philosophy and psychology we are still obliged to make value judgments. Without a metaphysical standpoint, without a reliable boundary marker between sanity and madness, we are still obliged to make decisions.

Such valorization of this fallen world is given by soap actress Sandra Bernhard when she writes, "Love is the only shocking act left on the face of the earth."[172] Surveying the madness of private lives and collective politics, she notes that, nonetheless,

> In the quietest night with whispers of tenderness and trust penetrating the senses, control, power, anger are thrown aside and we bear witness to the only valid instant in the universe, love.[173]

Her invocation is not sentimental, nor is it escapist. Love is a miraculous survivor of civil wars, outer and inner. Amid the savannas of the soul, the weary and battered heart springs anew to the summons of life. Each of us has questions to ask and answer in very private ways. Each question serves to stir the sediment below. (The etymology of *analysis* is not to dissect but to stir, loosen up.) Each question serves to bring to the surface elements of the personal myth, the implicit values shaping one's daily life.

What is your life's vocation or "calling" (as opposed to source of economic livelihood)? When did your childhood end? When did you leave home? *Have* you left home? How do your dependencies manifest? How do you repeatedly hurt yourself, undermine yourself? Where are you stuck in your journey? How are you still carrying Mother, Father? What fears block you? What is the unlived life that haunts you? What, on the invisible plane, supports your life on the visible plane?

---

[172] *Love, Love, and Love,* p. 7.

[173] Ibid., p. 8.

These questions are ineluctable, inescapable, imperative for a responsible, conscious life. If not consciously addressed, daily life carries far too great a burden of sadness. This Saturnian weight derives from the soul's distress. Or so we intuit. Thus we are painted into a corner—obliged to live more consciously lest we collude with and compound that wounding which fate has already given, and yet knowing no ground on which to plant the ego's flag, no rich West Indies of the Soul to claim for the Old World sovereign.

Let us return for a moment to Abe Lincoln, the Great Emancipator. If ever there was a large-souled person who lived with humor and sorrow in the real world, communed with noble ideas yet split rails, buried his children, sent men off to die, it was Lincoln. He had to carry his soul's heaviness, as we all do, and live in the world of daily duty, as we all do. What, then, was that talk of angels—"the better angels of our nature"—which might yet unify a sundered soul and a divided land? We all know his appeal was unsuccessful. Soon the nation, rent into North and South, was to sing around campfires, "Many are the hearts which are weary tonight / tenting on the old camp ground."[174] Yet his appeal was profound and represents an idea that may yet save us.

In the simple sentence with which he concluded the First Inaugural Address, there are critical words that demand close scrutiny. We recall that the medieval philosophers made much of *natura naturata* and *natura naturans,* nature natured and nature naturing. It is at the heart of the essentialist leap of faith that there is a given nature which is naturing through us whether we are conscious of it or not. Nature has a largeness of purpose and expresses its will through affective invasions, somatic symptoms and the dreams that inhabit sleep. But we must also note that modest word *our,* for it is *our* nature we are experiencing, incarnating. Surely we will find greater courage to live out our individuation when we recall that never before in history has there been such capacity for consciousness as we each represent, and no one of us will ever be here again. So this is the call, then, to be oneself, as a service to the whole of nature and to succeeding generations who depend on us to become ourselves.

---

[174] This song was sung to me by my grandmother, some of whose ancestors had sat around those fires. The song's title is "Tenting Tonight."

The notion of angels strikes us as quaint, even superstitious, but recall that the word angel comes from Greek *angelos,* messenger. We are flooded with messengers, perhaps all too many. Yet such visitations are precisely what we need to navigate the perilous rapids of the journey. In his 1939 talk, "The Symbolic Life," Jung commented that we have forgotten what our ancestors knew, that the silence is not silent, that the dark is luminous for those who wait upon it. When we attend the silence, wait upon the darkness, we find a wondrous brilliance and a presence which means that we are never wholly alone. Lame Deer, the Sioux medicine man, wrote,

> We Sioux believe that there is something within us that controls us, something like a second person almost. We call it *nagi,* what other people might call soul, spirit, or essence. One can't see it, feel it or taste it, but that time on the hill—and only that once—I knew it was there inside of me. Then I felt the power surge through me like a flood. I cannot describe it, but it filled all of me. Now I knew for sure that I would become a *wicasa wakan,* a medicine man.[175]

To attend the better angels of our nature, then, is to recover what people like Lame Deer knew and trusted, and to work toward healing the civil split within.

Our vision is opaque; we have painted ourselves into corners from which there is no escape, only sticky solutions. The sum of philosophical and psychological thinking over the last few centuries has ruled out the possibility of absolute or even objective knowledge. Thus, we are repeatedly facing the distress of Abraham. A voice tells us to slay our child, which can be anything we cherish. Is this the voice of God or of a complex—a mad, split-off part that possesses us? How can one ever know? In this condition we are still obliged to live concretely and responsibly, and hopefully as persons of value. Without a metaphysical Greenwich of the soul, how can we find the mythic referents that give us a sense of place? What longitudes and latitudes may be discerned? That great sea-traveler Newton could use reason and observation as his sextant and astrolabe. Today we suspect those instruments. And so we find ourselves adrift in angst and uncertainty.

---

[175] *Lame Deer: Seeker of Visions,* p. 6.

Perhaps the only gambit left is to see the world, in the Hindu metaphor, as "God's play." If we are obliged to play a game without absolute knowledge of its nature and rules, if winning and losing are illusions, then surely the purpose of the game is play itself. If our nervous ego can stand the ambiguity, the tension of opposites, the mystery of the messengers may be celebrated. As Helen Luke wrote of our understandable desire to hasten the end of our suffering,

> You shouldn't fight a neurosis in order to get rid of it. It is probably the one thing that is necessary for you to learn what is the matter. It is, therefore, the gift of God.[176]

Similarly, Gurdjieff counseled,

> Remember, you've come here having already understood the necessity of struggling with yourself—only with yourself. Therefore, thank everyone who gives you the opportunity.[177]

Obliged as we are to live without absolute knowledge, to live with a burdening past that invades and disrupts our intentions in the present, and unsupported by the great mythic institutions of the past, we are called to relinquish the ego's need for certainty, and to experience, even enjoy, the ambiguity of our condition. At least it is interesting. Accordingly, rather than say, "I am this construct, this ideology, this ego-identification," one may say, "I am my journey," or, "I am my dialogue with the angels, the messengers of mystery." The widest opening to this mystery occurs at the point of greatest peril and pain. Where we most want knowledge is where we are most vulnerable. To risk that vulnerability, to embrace the ambiguity, is to be free and radically open to the mystery that animated the myths of our ancestors.

Even today, Lincoln's summons remains—to attend the mystic chords of memory and trust the better angels of our nature. That is our myth.

---

[176] *Woman: Earth and Spirit,* p. 41.
[177] *Meetings with Remarkable Men,* p. 293.

Afterword
Heart-Work on All of the Images

This review of the place of myth in modern life is intended to articulate our challenge, which is to live consciously in a world without clear and sustaining mythic images.

As we have noted, it is not that the mythic energies are absent; it is rather that most of their still available vessels are exhausted and no longer have the power to mediate the mystery for us, or have become reified as ideologies, dogmas, fundamentalist idolatries. Other energies have slipped back into the unconscious and are as near as tonight's dream which, if attended faithfully, will offer precisely that mythic relocation we seek. As Augustine noted, "That which thou seekest is near, and already coming to meet thee."[178] And Friedrich Hölderlin wrote at the beginning of the nineteenth century,

> The gods are near, but difficult to grasp.
> But where danger is greatest,
> There deliverance also grows.[179]

Paradoxically, never have humans been more free. Yes, the loss of mythic grounding has tossed souls on the high seas and left them neurotic, addictive and adrift. Yet the threat of the abyss also brings a radical openness to the experience of being. Ironically, to experience this life in new ways it is necessary to recover what myth has represented historically.

While it is not our intent to seek to revive old myths, to artificially pump air into deflated images, it is necessary to review them, for each incarnates some timeless question, some recurrent human situation. To read the old myths and watch our feelings is a useful exercise. Some of those images will leave us cold, others will cause an inner stir. When such resonance occurs, we may be sure the myth has touched something very personal in us. Yeats once wrote that he had a coat made for himself to wear in the

---

[178] See above, p. 106.
[179] "Hymn to Patmos" (author's translation).

storms of our time and that his coat was a patchwork of mythologies. He meant, of course, that he had reread the old stories and stitched together the resonant parts and that they served him well in this time between the gods. James Hillman has directly asked us:

> Remember: what the Greeks said their Gods asked for above all else, and perhaps only, was not blood; it was not to be forgotten, that is, to be kept in mind, recollected as *psychological facts*. . . .
> [The God's] reality can never fade as long as they are remembered, that is, kept in *mind.* That's how they survive.[180]

Similarly, we are called to reread the world around us, and this includes the daily dance of images provided by the newspaper, by television and by pop culture. The gods are never far away. In Rilke's words,

> O gods, gods!
> who used to come so often and are still
> asleep in the Things around us. . . .
> Once again let it be your morning, gods.[181]

When we begin to read the world anew, we see that there are spiritual currents in all things, even the most banal. There are energies which, coming from below, drive and distort the culture. Using the Jungian principle of compensation, we can often see the pathologies of our time, both personal and collective, as the outer compensation for the inner wound. We may then understand our wounded comrades rather than judge them. And we will find that the world is a very rich place. An old Kabbalist saying has it, "There is another world, and this is it. "

Lastly, we must realize that the burden of meaning has truly shifted to our own shoulders. As obvious as this may seem, the import is enormous. We are required to accept that there is no parent to lead the way, no guru, no ideology to save us from the complexity and ambiguity of life. The measure of our personal development will hinge on two factors: our willingness to accept responsibility for finding our own myth, and our ability to sustain the ambiguity that always precedes a new experience of meaning. This task is critical for the health of both individual and society.

---

[180] "Once More into the Fray," pp. 5, 18.
[181] "Now It Is Time That Gods Came Walking Out," in *The Selected Poetry of Rainer Maria Rilke,* p. 277.

Myth is not created. It is experienced as an energy of the cosmos, shaped and incarnated by the unconscious, received or ignored by consciousness. The energy enters the image awhile, points toward the mystery, and then, when we wish to freeze and hold it, slips away, goes underground, and reappears in entirely new guise.

The single biggest shift in human culture, that which denotes the nature of modernism, is that the world has become psychological; that is, the logos or meaning of soul is everywhere manifest. This means that we have lost both simple beliefs and external authorities and are driven to recognize that the same energies driving the cosmos also course within. Myth tells us what is happening in us, in the unconscious. The meeting point of outer and inner is the individual psyche. This is where the newly formed myth will be found. Yes, it is difficult to accept this level of spiritual responsibility, hard to sustain the concomitant angst and attend the emergence of the new myth that comes from below—below history, below culture, below consciousness. Yet that is the task. As Sogyal Rinpoche writes:

> Looking in will require of us great subtlety and great courage—nothing less than a complete shift in our attitude to life and to the mind. We are so addicted to looking outside ourselves that we have lost access to our inner being almost completely. We are terrified to look inward, because our culture has given us no idea of what we will find. We may even think that if we do we will be in danger of madness. This is one of the last and most resourceful ploys of ego to prevent us from discovering our real nature.[182]

If we can accept the premise that nature brought us into life prepared to live it, that what we need is already coming to meet us, and that this trust and attendance upon the invisible world will take us where we need to go, then we shall always have a home. And our home is not a place or an ideology, it is the journey. In the words of Paul, we must remember that "it is not you that sustains the root: the root sustains you."[183] To know that the root of the soul reaches deeply down into the archetypal realm is to feel the invisible plane that supports the visible.

In his book *Fire in the Belly*, Sam Keen quotes a former professor of his who after reading the concluding journal entries of Admiral Byrd,

[182] *The Tibetan Book of Living and Dying*, p. 52.
[183] Rom. 11: 18, Authorized Version.

written in the wastes of the South Pole, asked the question,

> If you were alone, a thousand miles from any other person, fifty degrees below zero, and you were dying, what would have had to have happened to you to allow you to die with integrity and a sense of completion?[184]

It is my belief that we would need to feel two things: that we had lived our own life as well and as fully as possible, and that we had some linkage with a larger order of meaning, some connection with the mystery that courses through history and animates the individual soul.

These twin tasks—to live one's own life and to serve the mystery—are, paradoxically, aspects of the same thing, for the former obliges not only a willingness to accept responsibility for the course of one's life and for the meaning it embodies, but also the right to experience the absolutely different path it may take from those who have gone before. To reach the end of one's life and to know that one has not truly taken the journey is more terrible than any terrors one would have had to face on the way.

To feel that linkage to the larger order of things, a linkage by way of relationship, by way of meaningful social engagement, by way of wonder and terror at the forces of nature, by way of dream work and dialogue with the splintered psyche, is to experience the paradox that by the humble task of simply being ourselves we are thus more than ourselves. Then, in a time when the gods seem to have gone away, we may nonetheless glimpse the divine.

The task of healing is an alchemical work. It requires the mind, but it is not of the mind. It requires the activity of consciousness, but it transcends the intellect. Soul work is mythwork.

> Work of the eyes is done, now
> go and do heart-work
> on all of the images imprisoned within you; for you
> overpowered them. . . . Learn . . .
> the not yet beloved form.[185]

---

184 *Fire in the Belly*, p. 158.
185 "Turning Point," in *The Selected Poetry of Rainer Maria Rilke*, p. 135.

Bibliography

Adams, Hazzard, ed. *Critical Theory Since Plato.* New York: Harcourt, Brace, Jovanovich, 1970.

Alighieri, Dante Gabriel. *The Comedy of Dante Alighieri.* Trans. Dorothy Sayers. New York: Basic Books, 1963.

Arendt, Hannah. *Eichmann in Jerusalem.* New York: Peter Smith, 1983.

Ariette, Silvano. *Interpretation of Schizophrenia.* New York: Simon and Schuster, 1974.

Arnold, Matthew. *Poetry and Criticism of Matthew Arnold.* Ed. A. Dwight Culler. New York: Houghton, Mifflin, 1961.

Auden, W.H. *Collected Poems.* New York: Random House, 1976.

Augustine, St. *Confessions.* Trans. Vernon Bourke. Washington, DC: Catholic University Press, 1953.

Baynes, H.G. *Mythology of the Soul.* London, 1940.

Bernhard, Sandra. *Love, Love and Love.* New York: HarperCollins, 1993.

Berryman, John. *The Dispossessed.* New York: Noonday, 1948.

Bly, Robert; Hillman, James; and Meade, Michael, eds. *The Rag and Bone Shop of the Heart.* New York: HarperCollins, 1992.

Bonhoeffer, Dietrich. *Letters and Papers from Prison.* New York: MacMillan, 1972.

Brecht, Berthold. *Galileo.* New York: Grove, 1966.

Calasso, Robert. *The Marriage of Cadmus and Harmony.* New York: Alfred A. Knopf, 1993.

Campbell, Joseph. *The Masks of God.* 4 vols. New York: Penguin Books, 1976.

_____. *The Mythic Image* (Bollingen Series C). Princeton: Princeton University Press, 1974.

_____. *Myths To Live By.* New York: Bantam, 1972.

_____. *The Power of Myth.* Toronto: Doubleday, 1988.

_____. *This Business of the Gods . . .* Conversations with Fraser Boa. Caledon East, ON: Windrose Films Ltd., 1989.

Camus, Albert. *The Fall.* Trans. Justin O'Brien. New York: Vintage Books, 1956.

Conrad, Joseph. *The Heart of Darkness*. Ed. Robert Kimbrough. New York: W.W. Norton, 1963.

Dostoyevsky, Fyodor. *Notes from Underground*. New York: New American Library, 1961.

Durant, Will. *The Story of Philosophy*. New York: Washington Square Press, 1961.

Edinger, Edward F. *Transformation of the God-Image: An Elucidation of Jung's Answer to Job*. Toronto: Inner City Books, 1992.

Eliot, T.S. *The Complete Poems and Plays of T.S. Eliot*. New York: Harcourt, Brace, and World, 1952.

Ellman, Richard, and O'Clair, Robert, eds. *Modern Poems*. New York: W.W. Norton, 1976.

Flaubert, Gustave. *Madame Bovary*. Trans. Paul Le Man. New York: W.W. Norton, 1965.

Flores, Angel, trans. *An Anthology of French Poetry from de Nerval to Valéry*. New York: Doubleday Anchor, 1962.

_____. *An Anthology of German Poetry from Hölderlin to Rilke*. New York: Doubleday Anchor, 1960.

Forest, Jim. *Living with Wisdom*. Maryknoll, NY: Orbis Books, 1991.

Fromm, Erich. *Psychoanalysis and Religion*. New Haven: Yale University Press, 1990.

Frye, Northrop. *Fearful Symmetry: A Study of William Blake*. Boston: Beacon Press, 1947.

Fuller, Simon, ed., *The Poetry of War, 1914-1989*. London: BBC Books and Longman Group UK Limited, 1989.

Goethe, Johann Wolfgang von. *Faust*. Trans. Walter Kaufmann. New York: Anchor, 1962.

Goldenburg, Naomi. *Changing of the Gods*. New York: Beacon Press, 1979.

Gurdjieff, G.I. *Meetings with Remarkable Men*. New York: E.P. Dutton and Co., 1969.

Harding, M. Esther. *Woman's Mysteries, Ancient and Modern*. New York: Harper & Row, 1976.

Heidegger, Martin. *Existence and Being*. Trans. Werner Brock. Chicago: Henry Regnery, 1949.

Hillman, James. "Once More into the Fray." In *Spring 1994*.

Hobbes, Thomas. *Selections*. New York: Scribners, 1930.

Hollis, James. *Harold Pinter: The Poetics of Silence.* Carbondale, IL: Southern Illinois University Press, 1971.

———. *The Middle Passage: From Misery to Meaning in Midlife.* Toronto: Inner City Books, 1993.

———. *Under Saturn's Shadow: The Wounding and Healing of Men.* Toronto: Inner City Books, 1994.

Hopkins, Gerard Manley. *The Poems of Gerard Manley Hopkins.* New York: Oxford University Press, 1970.

The I Ching or Book of Changes. Trans. Richard Wilhelm. Rendered into English by Cary F. Baynes. Princeton: Princeton University Press, 1971.

James, William. *The Varieties of Religious Experience.* New York: Viking, 1982.

Jaspers, Karl. *Philosophy and the World.* New York: Regnery, 1989.

Jordan, Michael. *Encyclopedia of the Gods.* New York: Facts on File Books, 1993.

Joyce, James. *The Portable James Joyce.* New York: Viking, 1976.

Jung, C.G. *The Collected Works* (Bollingen Series XX). 20 vols. Trans. R.F.C. Hull. Ed. H. Read, M. Fordham, G. Adler, Wm. McGuire. Princeton: Princeton University Press, 1953-1979.

———. *Letters* (Bollingen Series XCV). 2 vols. Princeton: Princeton University Press, 1973.

———. *Memories, Dreams, Reflections.* Ed. Aniela Jaffé. New York: Random House, 1963.

Kafka, Franz. *Selected Short Stories of Franz Kafka.* Trans. Willa and Edwin Muir. New York: The Modern Library, 1952.

Keen, Sam. *Fire in the Belly.* Toronto: Bantam, 1991.

Kierkegaard, Sören. *Concluding Unscientific Postscript.* Ed. Howard Hong and Edna Hong. Princeton: Princeton University Press, 1992.

Laing, R.D. *The Politics of Experience.* New York: Ballantine, 1981.

Lame Deer. *Lame Deer: Seeker of Visions.* New York: Washington Square Press, 1972.

Lessing, Gotthold. *Lessing's Theological Writings.* Trans. Henry Chadwick. Stanford: Stanford University Press, 1957.

Levi-Strauss, Claude. *Savage Mind.* Chicago: University of Chicago Press, 1968.

Lincoln, Abraham. *Selected Speeches and Writings.* New York: Random, 1992.

Luke, Helen. *Woman: Earth and Spirit.* New York: Crossroads, 1984.

Mann, Thomas, *The Magic Mountain.* Trans. H.T. Lowe-Porter. New York: Modern Library, 1952.

Marlowe, Christopher. *The Tragical History of Dr. Faustus.* Ed. Fredrick Boas. New York: Gordian Press, 1966.

Merton, Thomas. *Thomas Merton: Spiritual Master.* Ed. Laurence Cunningham. Mahwah, NJ: Paulist Press, 1992.

The New English Bible. New York: Oxford University Press, 1972.

Nietzsche, Friedrich. *The Portable Nietzsche.* Ed. Walter Kaufmann. New York: Viking, 1972.

Norton Anthology of Poetry. Ed. A. Alison. New York: W.W. Norton, 1970.

The Oxford Dictionary of Quotations. Toronto: Oxford University Press, 1980.

Pagels, Elaine. *The Gnostic Gospels.* New York: Vintage Books, 1981.

Pascal, Blaise. *Pensées.* New York: E.P. Dutton and Co., 1958.

Perry, John Weir. *The Far Side of Madness.* Englewood Cliffs, NJ: Prentice-Hall, 1974.

Rilke, Rainer Maria. *Duino Elegies.* Trans. J.B. Leishman and Stephen Spender. New York: Norton, 1967.

_____. *The Selected Poetry of Rainer Maria Rilke.* Trans. Stephen Mitchell. New York: Vintage, 1989.

Rinpoche, Sogyal. *The Tibetan Book of Living and Dying.* San Francisco: Harper, 1992.

Rumi, Jelaluddin. *Feeling the Shoulder of the Lion: Poems and Teaching Stories.* Trans. Coleman Barks. Threshhold, VT: Threshhold Press, 1991.

Shakespeare, William. *The Complete Works of Shakespeare.* Glenview, IL: Scott-Foresman & Co., 1973.

Sharp, Daryl. *The Secret Raven: Conflict and Transformation in the Life of Franz Kafka.* Toronto: Inner City Books, 1980.

_____. *Personality Types: Jung's Model of Typology.* Toronto: Inner City Books, 1987.

_____. *Jung Lexicon: A Primer of Terms and Concepts.* Toronto: Inner City Books, 1991.

_____. *Who Am I, Really? Personality, Soul and Individuation.* Toronto: Inner City Books, 1995.

Sophocles. *Oedipus the King.* Trans. David Grene. Chicago: University of Chicago Press, 1960.

Steiner, George. *Language and Silence: Essays on Language, Literature and the Inhuman.* New York: Atheneum, 1976.

Tillich, Paul. *Theology of Culture.* Oxford: Oxford University Press, 1959.

Trudeau, Noah Andre. *Out of the Storm.* New York: Little Brown, 1994.

von Franz, Marie-Louise. *Alchemical Active Imagination.* Irving, TX: Spring Publications, 1979.

Wheelwright, Philip. *The Burning Fountain: A Study in the Language of Symbolism.* New York: Peter Smith, 1966.

Willey, Basil. *Nineteenth Century Studies: Coleridge to Matthew Arnold.* New York: Harper, 1966.

Yeats, William Butler. *The Collected Poems of W.B. Yeats.* New York: MacMillan, 1963.

Index

155

ALSO BY JAMES HOLLIS IN THIS SERIES

The Middle Passage: From Misery to Meaning in Midlife
ISBN 978-0-919123-60-1. (1993) 128 pp. $25

Under Saturn's Shadow: The Wounding and Healing of Men
ISBN 978-0-919123-64-9. (1994) 144 pp. $25

Write or phone for complete Catalogue of over 140 titles

INNER CITY BOOKS

Studies in Jungian Psychology by Jungian Analysts

53 Alvin Avenue, Toronto, ON M4T 2A8, Canada   (416) 927-0355
www.innercitybooks.net   booksales@innercitybooks.net